What others are saying

Tim and Tami Thurber's *Handing It Down* is an extraordinary accomplishment. They have taken the deep truths of Scripture and Christian doctrine and put them in language that faithfully communicates to families and children. There is no more important role than passing on the faith to our children. The Thurbers have offered a precious gift, based on their own commitment to Scripture and experience as parents. Their book is a welcome tool for teaching the unchanging truths of biblical faith to our children and grandchildren. Nothing is watered down, yet everything is accessible. This is a much needed volume for parents and grandparents. I highly recommend it.

— **Douglas R. Cullum, PhD,** Academic Vice President and Dean, Professor of Historical and Pastoral Theology, Northeastern Seminary, Rochester, NY 14624 • www.nes.edu

* * *

Raising godly children is not the youth pastor's job, it's the parents' job. Tim and Tami Thurber have given us an excellent, practical tool to help parents navigate their way through complex doctrines so they can be taught to children in an easy-to-understand way. I recommend this to any and every parent of younger children!

— **Bob Sjogren,** President, UnveilinGLORY

* * *

As a Christian parent, you pour into your children's spiritual lives from the time they are conceived. You pray over them, sing over them, take them to church, read them Bible stories. Then one day you wonder—did they really "get it"? Is there some major truth that was overlooked or skipped unintentionally along the way? Tim & Tami Thurber's book, *Handing It Down*, will take away the mystery by giving you a tool to talk to your children in a short daily devotional that imparts insight and ignites discussion.

— **C. Hope Flinchbaugh,** CEO, History Maker Publishing, Inc. Camp Hill, PA • www.historymakerpublishing.com

Scripture tells us in Deuteronomy 4:10b, that we are to pass on God's truth to our children.

> *Assemble the people before me to hear my words so that they may learn to revere me as long as they live in the land and may teach them to their children.*

More than ever, parents need to teach their kids who Jesus is and how to walk with Him before they are influenced by the world's values.

Unfortunately, most Christian parents do not feel equipped to adequately train their children at home. *Handing It Down* gives Christian parents the tools they need to impart biblical truth to their children. By using this study, children will learn more about God's Word, grow in their faith, and be able to stand in the face of trials.

— **Eric Foster,** Author, Dad

* * *

As a Chinese, I think *Handing It Down*, by Tim and Tami Thurber, is excellent for Chinese Christians because in China there are so many heresies.

With *Handing It Down* and with their parents' help, children will be able to spend time digesting and absorbing truth. This message will become imbedded in their young hearts and help produce God-fearing personalities.

This book provides verses for the whole family to read and memorize together, has many questions for the family to discuss, and it induces young minds to think. It also has many fun activities for the family to do and enjoy together.

— **Jane Moe,** Coordinator East Asia, SuperDoc

The most significant thing that parents can do for their children is to pass on their faith. Children need to be discipled. Tim & Tami Thurber have provided this excellent resource to help. In a world where many people believe there is no truth, this book establishes a firm foundation to help teach children biblical truth in a very practical way.

The Thurbers are excellent communicators. They understand that what we do is determined by who we are, which is formed by knowing God. There is a crisis of biblical illiteracy in the church. This book will help parents, Sunday school teachers or youth workers pass on theological truth in a very understandable way. All of God's truth is applicable to life. This book looks at the major doctrines of the Christian faith, explains them in understandable terms and shares applicable stories that can be used to communicate God's truth to children.

I can wholeheartedly recommend this book, knowing it will be a blessing to you. It presents God's Word clearly and accurately and will be of great benefit to raising up the next generation. It will assist you as you are *Handing It Down*.

> — **Jim Fahringer,** Executive Director, Montrose Bible Conference

handing it down

TEACHING YOUR CHILDREN THE BASIC TRUTHS OF FAITH

TIM & TAMI THURBER

SONFIRE MEDIA
A PUBLISHING COMPANY
GALAX, VIRGINIA

Handing It Down

Published by Sonfire Media, LLC
972 East Stuart Drive PMB 232
Galax, VA 24333 USA

© 2012 by Tim & Tami Thurber
All rights reserved.
Printed and bound in the United States of America

All rights reserved by the author. No part of this book may be used or reproduced in any manner whatsoever without written permission except in the case of brief quotations used in articles and reviews. The author is responsible for all content.

Unless otherwise noted, all scripture comes from THE HOLY BIBLE, NEW INTERNATIONAL VERSION®, NIV® Copyright © 1973, 1978, 1984, 2011 by Biblica, Inc.™ Used by permission. All rights reserved worldwide.

Scripture quotations marked NLT are taken from the Holy Bible, New Living Translation, copyright © 1996, 2004, 2007 by Tyndale House Foundation. Used by permission of Tyndale House Publishers, Inc., Carol Stream, Illinois 60188. All rights reserved.

Scripture quotations marked NET are from the NET Bible. Copyright © 1996-2006 by Biblical Studies Press, L.L.C. All right reserved. Used by permission.

Scripture is also taken from LA BIBLIA DE LAS AMERICAS®, Copyright © 1986, 1995, 1997 by The Lockman Foundation. Used by permission.

Cover and interior book design by Larry W. Van Hoose

ISBN No. 978-0-9825773-7-0

Dedication

To our parents, Ron and Sherry, Jim and Mary. Thank you for all of the time, energy, and wisdom you used to hand down your beliefs.

To our children, Miriam, Ryan, and Caleb. The greatest gift we could give you is an understanding of the truths of Scripture. We are blessed to be your parents.

Contents

Acknowledgments		XIII
Introduction		XV
SECTION ONE:	DOCTRINE OF THE BIBLE	
Overview	Doctrine of the Bible	1
Teaching 1	The Bible Gives Us the Truth	2
Teaching 2	The Bible Is from God	5
Teaching 3	External Evidence for the Bible	8
Teaching 4	Internal Evidence for the Bible	12
Teaching 5	The Holy Spirit Illuminates the Bible	15
Teaching 6	The Bible Shows Us Salvation	19
Teaching 7	The Bible Gives Us Hope	22
Teaching 8	We Should Read the Bible	26
SECTION TWO:	DOCTRINE OF GOD	
Overview	Doctrine of God	31
Teaching 1	The Trinity	32
Teaching 2	God Is Sovereign	36
Teaching 3	God Is Holy	40
Teaching 4	God Is Jealous	44
Teaching 5	God Is Eternal	48

Teaching 6	God: Revealed through General Revelation	52
Teaching 7	God Planned Salvation	56
Teaching 8	God Is Love	59

SECTION THREE: DOCTRINE OF JESUS

Overview	Doctrine of Jesus	65
Teaching 1	Jesus Is Fully God	66
Teaching 2	Jesus Is Fully Human	70
Teaching 3	Jesus Is the Payment	74
Teaching 4	Jesus' Death, for Us and for God	78
Teaching 5	Jesus' Resurrection	82
Teaching 6	Jesus Is Still Living	86
Teaching 7	Preparation for Jesus' Return	90
Teaching 8	Jesus Is the Crux	94
Teaching 9	Jesus Loves Us	98

SECTION FOUR: DOCTRINE OF THE HOLY SPIRIT

Overview	Doctrine of the Holy Spirit	103
Teaching 1	The Holy Spirit Is Fully God	104
Teaching 2	The Holy Spirit's Personhood	108
Teaching 3	The Holy Spirit Is throughout the Bible	112
Teaching 4	The Holy Spirit's Role in Salvation	115

Teaching 5	The Holy Spirit Living in Us	119
Teaching 6	The Holy Spirit Helps Us	122

SECTION FIVE: DOCTRINE OF PEOPLE

Overview	Doctrine of People	127
Teaching 1	People Were Created to Glorify God	129
Teaching 2	People Sin	133
Teaching 3	The Necessary Decision	138
Teaching 4	God's Commands for People	142
Teaching 5	The Ultimate Charge	146
Teaching 6	What Do People Get NOW?	151
Teaching 7	Life Is Hard	155

SECTION SIX: DOCTRINE OF THE CHURCH

Overview	Doctrine of the Church	161
Teaching 1	What Is the Church?	163
Teaching 2	Why Be Involved?	166
Teaching 3	The Enemy of the Church	171
Teaching 4	Your Duty toward the Church	175

Notes	183
Index of Terms	191

Acknowledgments

There are so many people we would like to thank for their encouragement and wisdom throughout this project. The idea for this book was conceived by Jim Thurber. Some of the illustrations are taken from the seminar he created, *Superdoc*. We thank him for his permission to use those ideas.

Ron and Sherry Zerbe, Dan and Bethany Zerbe and their family, and Carole and Russ Rigg gave invaluable advice and critique throughout the writing of this book.

Thank you also to Vie Herlocker and those at Sonfire Media who were excited about this project. We appreciate their encouragement, knowledge, and advice as they guided us through this process.

Our ultimate thanks goes to our Creator and Sustainer. We pray that this book will bring Him fame and glory.

Introduction

One definition of doctrine, according to the Merriam-Webster dictionary, is "something that is taught."[1] Thus, this devotional has come out of our desire to teach our own children basic truths of the Bible. It is amazing to hear our children's questions as they grapple with their faith while living in a world that challenges Christianity's fundamental beliefs. Our children are bombarded with opposing worldviews, and it is our job as parents to help them understand some basic doctrinal beliefs so they will stand firm. This book is a tool to help you teach the next generations.

When should you use these devotionals? That depends on your schedule. Some families sit down to breakfast together and like to jump-start the day with a family devotional. Others may want to use this at supper or right after supper. There is no perfect time that will automatically appear. Teaching the next generation should be a priority so we must *make* the time. However, don't get discouraged. There will be interruptions. There will be days when life gets too harried. The point is that you are teaching your children, and we pray that this tool will help.

Who should use these devotionals? We realize that each family will have a different level of understanding of biblical knowledge. We included two levels of instruction to help you individualize the lessons to meet the needs of your family. *Handing It Down* covers six doctrines—the Bible, God the Father, Jesus the Son, the Holy Spirit, People, and the Church—and each doctrine includes several teachings.

How this book is organized:

Overview

Each doctrine has an overview page to help you understand why we included the doctrine in this book. We included a theme verse that you can explain to your children and memorize as a family.

Digging Down

This section presents the most basic level of instruction. It includes a story, brief activity, or questions designed to introduce the topic and to help deepen your relationship as a family. When there is a passage of Scripture to read, we recommend that you look up the verses in the Bible so your children recognize the authority of the Bible. If your children are old enough to read, you may want to have one of them read the passage.

Digging Deeper

If you have children who are a little older or who already have grasped the basic teaching covered in "Digging Down," then you can include "Digging Deeper." You may read it on the same day as "Digging Down" or perhaps you will want to read that section the next day. This may also be used to enhance your own knowledge if you do not have older children. As in "Digging Down," you will benefit if you look up the Scripture passages in the Bible.

Family Fun

Occasionally, we will include a fun activity that your family can do together. Use these as you wish.

We will be praying for you as you use this tool to help you teach the next generation the timeless truths of the doctrines of the Bible, God the Father, Jesus the Son, the Holy Spirit, People, and the Church. May God bless you as you hand your faith down to the next generations.

Tim & Tami Thurber

SECTION 1

DOCTRINE OF THE BIBLE

OVERVIEW

What do your meals look like? Does your family like rice, pasta, or bread? Thankfully, our children like those foods, and so we try to have one of them at every dinner. We all cook a little differently, and our children all probably like different foods, but the one constant is that we do not want our children to go hungry. Often, as parents, we spend many hours a week on feeding our children physical food, but do we spend as much time nourishing them spiritually? This section will help you guide your children through understanding their spiritual bread, the Bible.

Our theme verse is found in both the Old Testament and the New Testament. Right before leading the Israelites into the Promised Land, God reminded them that he provided their food while they wandered through the desert for forty years. He said that they should look to him not *only* for their physical food, but for their spiritual food as well (Deut. 8:3). In the New Testament, Jesus quoted this verse after he had been without food for forty days, and Satan came to him, tempting him to turn a rock into bread (Matt. 4:4). Through his response, Jesus showed all of us that our spiritual food, which comes from the Bible, is just as important as our physical food.

Theme Verse for Memorization: Deuteronomy 8:3b NLT

People do not live by bread alone; rather we live by every word that comes from the mouth of the LORD.

Let's learn about our spiritual food.

Teaching 1: The Bible Gives Us the Truth

Review Theme Verse

People do not live by bread alone; rather we live by every word that comes from the mouth of the LORD. (Deuteronomy 8:3b NLT)

DIGGING DOWN

Do you know the verse John 3:16? Can you quote it? In English, it states, "For God so loved the world that he gave his one and only Son, that whoever believes in him shall not perish but have eternal life." However, English is not the only translation of the Bible! If you were to read that same verse in Spanish, it would read like this, "Porque de tal manera amó Dios al mundo, que dio a su Hijo unigénito, para que todo aquel que cree en El, no se pierda, mas tenga vida eterna." (La Biblia de las Américas) Although the English and Spanish sound different, they have the same true message.

Even though the Bible is translated into many different languages, it tells the same truth about who God is, what Jesus' life was like, and even about how much God loves you. But that is not all the Bible tells us! In fact, some people study the Bible their whole lives, and every time they read it they learn something new. Why do people study the Bible? Because they believe it is true. That's what the people in today's verses learned.

Look Up and Read Acts 17:10-12

> *As soon as it was night, the believers sent Paul and Silas away to Berea. On arriving there, they went to the Jewish synagogue. Now the Berean Jews were of more noble character than those in Thessalonica, for they received the message with great eagerness and examined the Scriptures every day to see if what Paul said was true. As a result, many of them believed, as did also a number of prominent Greek women and many Greek men.*

Paul and his friend Silas traveled around telling people about Jesus. The people in the town of Berea heard Paul and wondered if what he said was true. They knew the Bible was true, so they compared Paul's teaching with the Bible. As they studied the Bible, they found that Paul and Silas were right when they talked about Jesus, because the Bible said the same things.

Everyone needs to believe that something is true. Some people think their friends tell them the truth. Others say their government tells them the truth. Some people say a religion other than Christianity tells them the truth. Some even believe that each person can come up with his or her own truth. As Christians we believe that the Bible is true, and so whenever we hear anything, whether it is from our government, our friends, or another religion, we must do as the Bereans did and find out if what we hear agrees with what the Bible says.

You know, it does not matter what language the Bible is translated into, whether it is Spanish, Chinese, Swahili, or some other language. If it is the Bible, then it is true. There will be people who will tell you that they know the truth, but if their truth is different from the Bible, then we know that what they say is wrong. Let's be like the Bereans and study the Bible, and then we will know the truth.

Questions

1. What did the Bereans do to find out if what Paul and Silas said was true?

2. What are places, besides the Bible, where people might look to find out if something is true?

3. Where would we look to find out if something is true?

4. What are some things you have heard people say are true? Do those things agree with the Bible?

Digging Deeper

In our time, there is a fallacy that there are many truths. I can believe my truth, you can believe your truth, and we are supposed to accept each other's truths (and thus, interestingly, we do not engage in conversation about what truth may be because we do not want to disagree with anyone). But we must ask, how can we all have different truths? Isn't the nature of "truth" something that MUST be correct? I cannot pronounce that we are both telling the truth if I state that it is okay to steal while you say that stealing is wrong. It cannot be true that stealing is both right and wrong. In other words, both you and I cannot be correct if we are saying opposite things. Only one of the statements can be true. So, how do we find what is true?

We believe we should rely on the Bible, not on people, to determine truth. Why? Because people change, and people make wrong decisions. We don't even need to look at extreme examples such as Hitler to realize that people sometimes believe they know truth when they obviously do not. Look at yourself. Did you believe in Santa, only to find out years later that your truth about where Christmas presents come from was based on faulty information? Because we cannot know everything about the universe, we will always base our personal truth on faulty information.

Look Up and Read Isaiah 45:18-19

> For this is what the LORD says— he who created the heavens, he is God; he who fashioned and made the earth, he founded it; he did not create it to be empty, but formed it to be inhabited—he says: "I am the LORD, and there is no other. I have not spoken in secret, from somewhere in a land of darkness; I have not said to Jacob's descendants, 'Seek me in vain.' I, the LORD, speak the truth; I declare what is right."

The Bible comes from a God who states that he tells the truth. Not only that, but this same God who wants to give us truth is also the one who created the world. If we are living in God's created universe, then he must know the truth about it. Thankfully, he did not leave us floundering to find the truth in our universe. He gave us the Bible.

Did you know that when Jesus was teaching he often included the words, "I tell you the truth"? Count it up (in Matthew's gospel alone, we counted twenty-nine times when Jesus said, "I tell you the truth"). Truth matters to God. It makes sense that we get our truth from him.

Teaching 2: The Bible Is from God

Review Theme Verse

> People do not live by bread alone; rather we live by every word that comes from the mouth of the LORD. (Deuteronomy 8:3b NLT)

DIGGING DOWN

Pretend you are going to blow up a balloon. Grab the balloon in your hand, raise it to your lips, and then, what do you do? Fill your lungs with air so you can blow it into the balloon. What happens to the balloon as you breathe air into it? It slowly gets bigger.

What did the balloon look like before you blew any air into it? Did you describe it as flat, floppy, or unimpressive? A balloon that has not been blown up is not really good for anything. However, after you breathed air into it, the balloon can be used as a toy for hitting in the air or as a decoration at a party. Your breath gave the balloon beauty and made it useful. When we think about the air you put into the balloon, we will understand a little more about why we say the Bible came from God.

> God did not merely dictate words or propositions to passive authors, but rather he impacted personally their whole beings, allowing them actively to comprehend, interpret, and convey his will to others according to the limitations of their understanding and language.
> - Theodore Stylianopoulos[1]

Look Up and Read 2 Timothy 3:16-17

> All Scripture is God-breathed and is useful for teaching, rebuking, correcting and training in righteousness, so that the servant of God may be thoroughly equipped for every good work.

How did the writer of 2 Timothy describe Scripture (which is the Bible)? Some translations say "inspired by God" others say "God-breathed."[2] They both mean the same thing because "inspired" means "God-breathed." So, we believe the Bible has meaning because it came from God. Now, that does not mean that God sat down with a pencil and paper and wrote the Bible and then sent it to earth on a spaceship. God did not do that. God used people to write the Bible. However, we believe that the Bible came from God because we believe he carefully chose the people he wanted to write it. Then, as the person wrote, God breathed his message into the person. Without God's breathing into it, the Bible would just be another book that people wrote.

Think back to our pretend balloon. You needed to breathe your air into it so it became useful. That is like God breathing his message into the minds of men who then wrote it down. The Bible came from God, and because he breathed into it, it has a purpose. We use it to teach about God, to show people where they are sinning, and to explain to people how to follow God. It is useful because it is inspired, or God-breathed. Next time you wonder if the Bible came from God, think about a balloon.

Questions

1. Why do we say that the Bible came from God?
2. Did God pick up a pencil and write the Bible himself?
3. What does "inspired" mean?
4. What can we use the Bible for?

DIGGING DEEPER

The Bible was written by human authors who were breathed into by God. This could be a confusing concept. Theodore Stylianopoulos explains it well (see the quote on the previous page). Human authors were the ones who actually held the writing utensil and wrote the words. God chose the authors, and he breathed his message into them; yet each author's God-inspired writing reflects his own personality and even education level.

Look Up and Read 2 Peter 1:20-21

Above all, you must understand that no prophecy of Scripture came about by the prophet's own interpretation of things. For prophecy never had its origin in the human will, but prophets, though human, spoke from God as they were carried along by the Holy Spirit.

In Acts 27:15 Paul was caught in a major storm as he sailed along the coast of Crete. Unable to steer the ship because of the fierce winds, the sailors gave up fighting the storm and were "driven along" by the wind. This Greek word translated "driven along" in Acts is the same Greek word used in 2 Peter and translated "carried along" in the case of the prophet writing scripture.[3]

As the wind was the force that moved the ship, so the power of the Holy Spirit was the force that gave the human author the Word of God. This does not diminish the author's own personality, but it does mean the message, written by a human hand, came from God. Therefore, we can believe the Bible is a message from God for us today.

Teaching 3: External Evidence for the Bible

Review Theme Verse

People do not live by bread alone; rather we live by every word that comes from the mouth of the LORD. (Deuteronomy 8:3b NLT)

DIGGING DOWN

Where do you live? How long have you lived there? Do you know who lived there before you? Do you know who lived in your area one hundred years ago? How about one thousand years ago? In many areas of the world you can dig in the ground and find things such as pottery, ruins of buildings, or even parts of weapons that ancient civilizations used. These artifacts are one way that we find out about people who lived a long time ago. Archeologists dig up clues as to who lived and what their lives were like. In fact, some people refuse to believe anything is real or true unless they have these archeological clues. One example of people's need for archeological proof is how people used to doubt the existence of Pontius Pilate.

Look Up and Read Mark 15:1-5

> *Very early in the morning, the chief priests, with the elders, the teachers of the law and the whole Sanhedrin, made their plans. So they bound Jesus, led him away and handed him over to Pilate. "Are you the king of the Jews?" asked Pilate. "You have said so," Jesus replied. The chief priests accused him of many things. So again Pilate asked him, "Aren't you going to answer? See how many things they are accusing you of." But Jesus still made no reply, and Pilate was amazed.*

According to the Bible, Pontius Pilate was the Roman ruler who gave permission to crucify Jesus (Mark 15:15). However, for many years some people said the Bible was just a collection of made-up stories, and they pointed to Pontius Pilate as one of their proofs. No one had ever found any artifacts that mentioned Pontius Pilate; he was not even mentioned in any Roman documents. Therefore, people said that Christians just made up the Bible and included a story about a pretend person called Pontius Pilate who gave permission to crucify Jesus.

However, in 1961 a man named Dr. Frova led a group of Italian archeologists in a dig around an amphitheater near Caesarea-on-the-Sea in Israel. Do you know what he found? An ancient stone inscribed with Pontius Pilate's name![4] Because of that find, today most people agree that Pontius Pilate did exist. The Bible was telling true history. In fact, archeology continues to prove that the stories from the Bible are not made up legends, but that the people written about in the Bible really did exist. That's one reason why we believe the Bible is true.

Questions

1. Who was the Roman Ruler that we read about in the Bible, but who many people said did not exist?

2. Although some people used to say that Pontius Pilate did not exist, now people realize that he was a real person. Why did they change their mind?

3. What is one reason, from today's reading, why we believe the Bible is telling the truth?

Digging Deeper

One reason people say the Bible is full of errors is because it was written so long ago. They argue that, since the Bible has been copied and translated so often, the copies we have today must have radically changed from the first copies. However, there is external evidence, that is, proof found outside of the pages of the Bible, that shows us that what we read today is the same information that was written thousands of years ago.

In 1947, a Bedouin was looking for his lost goat among some caves near the Dead Sea in Israel. But what he discovered was far more important than his goat! He found jars with ancient manuscripts in them, dating back to around Jesus' time! After many more excavations, archaeologists discovered ancient fragments of all of the books of the Old Testament except Esther. These are called the Dead Sea Scrolls.[5] This was an important find because it was discovered that the fragments from the biblical Dead Sea Scrolls, although they were 1,000 years older than any copies that had been found before, matched up to what our Bible says today. Archeology helped to prove that the Bible has not become full of error through its many years of being copied and translated.

The Dead Sea Scrolls are fragments from the Old Testament, and we also have many copies of the New Testament. It is interesting that people who state that the Bible could not possibly be reliable have no difficulty accepting the reliability of other historical documents, even though only a few of those documents exist. Here is a chart with a few examples of documents that are considered reliable.[6]

Text	Oldest Manuscripts	Number Surviving
Pliny (wrote A.D. 61 – 113)	A.D. 850	7
Plato (wrote 427-347 B.C.)	A.D. 900	7
Suetonius (wrote A.D. 75 – 160)	A.D. 900	8
New Testament (written A.D. 50-100)	c. A.D. 130 and following	5,600

People do not argue whether the letters of Pliny were truly written by Pliny although we only have seven copies of these letters, and these seven copies are copies from seven hundred years after the original letters were written. Even though the evidence that Pliny actually wrote these letters is slim, their authenticity is not debated.

Plato is another example of a person whose writings are not debated, and yet the earliest copies that we have were written approximately one thousand three hundred years after Plato wrote the original manuscript. In fact, we have only seven copies of his writings that date that closely to the time in which he lived! And yet, we do not debate the existence of Plato or the veracity of his writings.

Compare those numbers to the statistics about the New Testament. We have over five thousand six hundred copies of manuscripts that come within one hundred years of when they were written, and yet some people argue that we do not have enough evidence to prove that they are reliable manuscripts! The external evidence of archaeology and the authenticity of the manuscripts themselves should help us realize that the Bible is true and reliable.

If you would like to learn more about some archeological finds that agree with the accounts of the Bible, look up these:

1. The Moabite Stone

2. The Siloam Inscription

Family Fun

You can modify these options to fit the ages and interests of your children.

1. Take some time to discover who used to live in your area, town, or even house. You may be able to use a local library, have a local history teacher or an older member of the community over for a meal, or go to the local government office to look at any records they might have. Not only will this give your children a sense of the history of which they are a part, but also it will give them an idea of how people can look for clues about history.

2. Bury a time-capsule in your yard. Place a few items such as a picture of your family, a daily newspaper, and/or a small New Testament in a container (preferably a bug proof and waterproof container). Bury this deep in your yard, knowing that you may be giving some future generation a glimpse at your life today.

Teaching 4: Internal Evidence for the Bible

Review Theme Verse

People do not live by bread alone; rather we live by every word that comes from the mouth of the LORD. (Deuteronomy 8:3b NLT)

Digging Down

Let's have a little fun. Have you ever played "telephone?" Try it now. The first person should think of a sentence, a phrase, or even a tongue twister. Then that person should whisper it in the second person's ear. The second person then whispers what he/she heard to the third person. Continue whispering the message until everyone has had a chance to hear it and tell someone else. Then ask the last person what he/she heard. The first person should then tell what was originally said (then everyone can share what he or she heard!). Were the beginning phrase and the ending phrase anything like each other? Usually they aren't, and the more sentences said or the harder the phrase, the more it gets confused. Did you notice, though, that at the end of the game the first person was able to tell everyone the original message?

Look Up and Read Luke 1:1-4

> *Many have undertaken to draw up an account of the things that have been fulfilled among us, just as they were handed down to us by those who from the first were eyewitnesses and servants of the word. With this in mind, since I myself have carefully investigated everything from the beginning, I too decided to write an orderly account for you, most excellent Theophilus, so that you may know the certainty of the things you have been taught.*

When Luke was writing the gospel of Luke, he wrote things that he heard people say about Jesus because he himself had never met Jesus. However, there was no problem finding many eyewitnesses to Jesus' life. These people had seen with their own eyes and heard with their own ears what Jesus did and said. Luke talked with these people, listened to their stories about Jesus, and then wrote down some of the things he heard.

Some people might say, "Well, how do we know that what Luke wrote was true?" Good question! If Luke were lying, the eyewitnesses would have corrected Luke, and no one would have believed what Luke wrote. At the end of the game "Telephone" that you played earlier, the first person corrected what the last person said. This is how the eyewitnesses would have corrected Luke.

This is another reason why we say the Bible is true. Since the eyewitnesses, those who actually had seen Jesus, agreed with the accounts, then we can believe them.

Questions

1. What is an eyewitness?

2. How would an eyewitness make sure that the Bible stories are true?

3. From today's reading, what is another reason why we say that the Bible is true?

DIGGING DEEPER

Besides the external, archaeological evidence that supports the Bible's claims, there is also internal evidence that the Bible is true. Internal evidence means that people in the Bible used the Bible as truth.

In the Old Testament, Daniel read Scripture to find truth. When he wanted to know how long his hometown of Jerusalem would be in ruins and the people would be in exile, Daniel turned to the Scriptures to find what God said.

Look Up and Read Daniel 9:2

> *In the first year of his reign, I, Daniel, understood from the Scriptures, according to the word of the LORD given to Jeremiah the prophet, that the desolation of Jerusalem would last seventy years.*

In the New Testament, Jesus often quoted scripture as truth. For every temptation that Jesus faced, he fought Satan by quoting Scripture. Jesus showed Satan the truth by quoting Scripture (Matt. 4:1-11) to him!

During his debates with the Jewish leaders, Paul often referred to the truth of Scripture (Acts 17:2, Gal. 3:8). Because these people, Daniel, Jesus, Paul, and others, believed that the Bible was true and not full of errors, then we can agree with them that it is true.

Even with this internal and external evidence, have you ever heard people say that the Bible is full of errors? If people say that to you, challenge them to tell you about one error. Chances are that they cannot. Many people use that excuse, but they have not studied the Bible enough to actually prove their statement.

And, if they do state something that they think is an error, you should spend time exploring it. Check what the Bible actually says. Check both external and internal evidence. Many times people hear something, but because they don't study it themselves, they misunderstand the issue and base their belief that the Bible is full of errors on faulty information.

When studied, the Bible's internal and external evidence show the truth of Scripture.

Teaching 5: The Holy Spirit Illuminates the Bible

Review Theme Verse

People do not live by bread alone; rather we live by every word that comes from the mouth of the LORD. (Deuteronomy 8:3b NLT)

Handing It Down

DIGGING DOWN

Choose a leader. Everyone sit so they can see that leader. Now, the leader should open the Bible and read the first verse that he or she sees. However, do not speak aloud; just "mouth" the words. The rest of the group should try to repeat the verse. How difficult was it to understand the mouthed words? If you have time, you can take turns being the leader.

This game helps us appreciate how the Holy Spirit aids us in understanding the Bible. Although we see the words on the page of the Bible or we hear someone reading it, sometimes we don't really understand what the Bible means. It doesn't seem to make sense. Thankfully, we are not alone as we try to figure out what the Bible says. The Holy Spirit helps us.

Look Up and Read 1 Corinthians 2:12-14

> *What we have received is not the spirit of the world, but the Spirit who is from God, so that we may understand what God has freely given us. This is what we speak, not in words taught us by human wisdom but in words taught by the Spirit, explaining spiritual realities with Spirit-taught words. The person without the Spirit does not accept the things that come from the Spirit of God but considers them foolishness, and cannot understand them because they are discerned only through the Spirit.*

Because the Bible is from God, God knows what it means. So, if we have trouble understanding the Bible, God is the best person to help us! When we are part of God's family, we have the Holy Spirit, who is God, with us to help us understand the Bible. In fact, these verses state that without the Holy Spirit, you would think that the Bible does not make any sense and is foolishness. Another word for helping to understand is to *illuminate*. Thus, we can say that the Holy Spirit illuminates Scripture.

If you wake up in the middle of the night and want a drink of water, you turn on a light. Otherwise, you would find yourself bumping into a table, knocking your head on a cabinet, or tripping over a rug. In the dark you would also have a difficult time finding a glass and the water faucet. You need light to illuminate the kitchen so you can easily understand where the table, cabinet, and rug are. You need light to help you understand where you left your glass and where the faucet is. The light is like the Holy Spirit.

The Holy Spirit illuminates the words of the Bible. We do not have to walk in the dark or read words that we cannot understand. When we read the Bible, we should ask the Holy Spirit to help us understand whatever God wants us to learn. When we do that, the Bible will not seem like someone mouthing words that we cannot understand. Instead, the Holy Spirit will illuminate what it means and thus we will understand what we are reading.

Questions

1. What does "illuminate" mean?
2. Who illuminates the Bible for us?
3. Why does the Bible seem like foolishness to some people?
4. What should we do before we read the Bible so that we can understand what God wants to teach us?

Digging Deeper

Poets often use images to help the reader understand their subject. For instance, Carl Sandburg's poem "Fog" begins, "The fog comes on

little cat feet."[7] Obviously this does not mean that fog actually grew feline feet, but rather that fog silently approaches.

The English language has many images that we use. If you were to read, "He is a chip off the old block," you would understand that someone's child is quite a bit like his father. You are not stating that the father is a three-dimensional cube of wood with a small piece missing. Nor are you commenting that the child is a ragged shred of splinters. You are merely using an image to help illustrate your point.

The Bible has many images associated with it. Sometimes these images are hard to understand, and thus we need the Holy Spirit to help us. Read the following verses and ask the Spirit to help you learn about the Bible by understanding the images used.

1. The Bible is a lamp: Psalm 119:105

   Your word is a lamp for my feet, a light on my path.

2. The Bible is a mirror: James 1:23-24

   Anyone who listens to the word but does not do what it says is like someone who looks at his face in a mirror and, after looking at himself, goes away and immediately forgets what he looks like.

3. The Bible is like bread: Deuteronomy 8:3

   He humbled you, causing you to hunger and then feeding you with manna, which neither you nor your ancestors had known, to teach you that man does not live on bread alone but on every word that comes from the mouth of the LORD.

4. The Bible is like honey & gold: Psalm 19:10

   They are more precious than gold, than much pure gold; they are sweeter than honey, than honey from the honeycomb.

The Bible is full of images, stories, truths, and promises that we should read to gain understanding about God, our world, and even ourselves.

However, it also can be confusing. Thankfully, we have the Holy Spirit who wants to help us understand what the Bible says. Sometimes the Holy Spirit teaches us as we pray, but there are other times when he teaches us by using other Christians.

Do you know a Christian you could ask about the Bible? The Holy Spirit often guides us to a person or book that will help illuminate Scripture. We should not be shy in asking for help from another Christian when we do not understand Scripture. When we ask for help, we are admitting that we desire to understand the Bible, and we are allowing the Holy Spirit to illuminate it for us.

Teaching 6: The Bible Shows Us Salvation

Review Theme Verse

People do not live by bread alone; rather we live by every word that comes from the mouth of the LORD. (Deuteronomy 8:3b NLT)

Digging Down

What is one book or movie that made you scared or glad? What is one that taught you something new? When authors write a movie or book, they do it for a purpose. Whether it is to make someone scared, to make someone happy, or to teach something, there is always a purpose. In today's verses we will read about one purpose of the Bible.

Look Up and Read John 20:30-31

Jesus performed many other signs in the presence of his disciples, which are not recorded in this book. But these are written that you may believe that Jesus is the Messiah, the Son of God, and that by believing you may have life in his name.

One of Jesus' best friends, John, wrote this book of the Bible. That is why it is named John! Here, near the end of the book, John gave his reason for writing. Look at these verses to find out why John wrote this book. John wrote down all about Jesus' life so that anyone who read what he wrote would understand who Jesus was and believe that Jesus did really live, die, and rise again. Jesus did really love. Jesus did really live a sinless life. Jesus did really take away our sins when he died. However, if the Bible had not been written, then we would have no idea who Jesus was, that he forgave our sins, and how to become part of his family. John wrote so that we can believe.

Why would we want to believe? Look at the verses in John again; they tell us we should believe so that we may have life in Jesus' name. In other words, we believe so that we become part of God's family.

Each one of us has a birth mom and dad. Some of us may also have an adopted mom or dad or maybe even a step-mom or step-dad. We are each part of a family. God says that, although we have a family here on earth, he also wants us to be part of his family. When we join his family, it is called being "born again" into his family (John 3). This "born again" life is the life that John says we get by believing in Jesus.

Isn't it great that God gave us the Bible so we can learn how to become part of his family? If we did not have the Bible, we would not know how to be born into the family of God. We can thank God for the gift of the Bible and the gift of being born again.

Questions

1. What is one purpose of the Bible that we just talked about?
2. In whom do we need to believe in order to get new life in God's family?

3. What is it called when we join God's family? (Hint: We were *born* into an earthly family.)

Digging Deeper

Have you ever heard of Jeremiah? He was one of the prophets to the nation of Judah (where the city of Jerusalem was) before and during their exile to Babylon. God revealed to Jeremiah the seriousness of Judah's sin against God. Read Jeremiah 36:1-3, to see what the Lord told Jeremiah to write.

> *In the fourth year of Jehoiakim son of Josiah king of Judah, this word came to Jeremiah from the LORD: "Take a scroll and write on it all the words I have spoken to you concerning Israel, Judah and all the other nations from the time I began speaking to you in the reign of Josiah till now. Perhaps when the people of Judah hear about every disaster I plan to inflict on them, they will each turn from their wicked ways; then I will forgive their wickedness and their sin."*

Then read Jeremiah 36:7 to see how Jeremiah hoped the people would respond.

> *Perhaps they will bring their petition before the LORD and will each turn from their wicked ways, for the anger and wrath pronounced against this people by the LORD are great.*

What did God reveal to Jeremiah? God takes sin very seriously, and here God revealed to Jeremiah the destruction and disaster that he would bring on Judah because they sinned. God wanted his people to turn away from their sin and turn back to him.

Do we take sin seriously? Some people say that they can sin because God is loving and will not condemn their sin. When people do that they are picking and choosing what part of God's words they want to believe. They want to believe that God loves them because that helps them. However, they refuse to believe that God also hates sin (Rom. 2:7-11). The Bible is not a book that we can pick and choose sections to believe. The entire Bible is God's truth to us. We must accept it all.

Some people do not seem to care if God dislikes sin or not. They say it is their right to live however they want; they don't care what God says. However, this passage in Jeremiah, along with many others in the Bible, reveals how much God dislikes sin. God does forgive, but only when we repent and turn away from sin (Luke 24:46-47). We cannot consciously sin and assume God does not care.

Unfortunately, the people that Jeremiah warned did not turn away from their sin. They continued not to care about God, and so God sent the army of Babylon into Judah to take them into exile. There is a punishment for sin, and if we choose to ignore God's hatred for sin, as the Jews did in Jeremiah's day, then we too might face the wrath of God (Rom. 1:17-19). The Bible tells us of the severity of our sin, and we must listen to its warnings.

Teaching 7: The Bible Gives Us Hope

Review Theme Verse

People do not live by bread alone; rather we live by every word that comes from the mouth of the LORD. (Deuteronomy 8:3b NLT)

DIGGING DOWN

Think of a time when someone was mean to you. What happened? How did you feel? Was this person mean only once or many times? Sometimes people are unkind to another person repeatedly. And, if you are the person being picked on, it does not feel good. In fact, you may go to school or the playground hoping that the mean person will not be there or that the person will not pick on you. Hope is a good thing. Did you know that one reason why God gave us the Bible is so that we have hope when people are being unkind?

Look Up and Read Romans 15:2-6

> *Each of us should please our neighbors for their good, to build them up. For even Christ did not please himself but as it is written: "The insults of those who insult you have fallen on me." For everything that was written in the past was written to teach us, so that through the endurance taught in the Scriptures and the encouragement they provide we might have hope. May the God who gives endurance and encouragement give you the same attitude of mind toward each other that Christ Jesus had, so that with one mind and one voice you may glorify the God and Father of our Lord Jesus Christ.*

The verses we just read say that sometimes people are mean. People do insult us and hurt us. However, when they are mean to us, who are they also being mean to (v. 3)? Do you think Jesus likes it when people are mean to us? Of course not! Now, we cannot assume God will take all of the unkind people out of our lives. However, because we are part of God's family, we can have hope. This comes when we read the Bible.

The verses we read also say that God gives encouragement, or comfort. When you get hurt, you may run to your mom or dad to help you feel better. We get comfort from our parents, and God wants our parents to comfort us. We can also get comfort from God. The next time someone picks on you, go to your mom or dad, but also try talking to God about it. He can give you comfort.

These verses also say that God gives endurance. This means that God will help you have the courage to keep going to school or the playground, even when someone may be unkind. Ask God to give you the courage you need, because he can do that!

The Bible does not say that life will be easy. It does not say that God will get rid of all the mean people in our lives, but the Bible is full of stories showing when God gave comfort and endurance to someone when they needed it. God is with us, too, when life seems hard. That is an amazing promise! God created the entire world, and yet he loves you enough to want to help you. That gives us hope!

Questions

1. When someone insults us, who are they also insulting?

2. Whom can you go to for comfort (to help you feel better)?

3. Where can we read stories of how God gave comfort and endurance to people?

Digging Deeper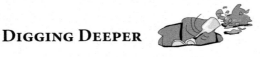

Because the Bible tells us of God's love and comfort, we have hope in difficult situations, including when someone is mean to us. However, you may declare that your problems are much deeper than someone being mean to you. The Bible tells us that God understands your problems. Even in the deepest, saddest, and most unfair situations, God does understand, and God can give you hope.

Have you ever read the story of Job? Job was a rich man who owned land and servants. He also had many children. If he were living today, we would say he had it all. However, the Bible says that suddenly his possessions were destroyed, and his children were killed. What a hopeless situation! In fact, Job gets so depressed that he asks God for death.

Look Up and Read Job 6:8-13

Oh, that I might have my request, that God would grant what I hope for, that God would be willing to crush me, to let loose his hand and cut off my life! Then I would still have this consolation— my joy in unrelenting pain—that I had not denied the words of the Holy One. What strength do I have, that I should still hope? What prospects, that I should be patient? Do I have the strength of stone? Is my flesh bronze? Do I have any power to help myself, now that success has been driven from me?

Job had no hope. Have you ever felt like that? Does anything in life ever feel hopeless? Thankfully, God gave us the Bible so we can read of Job who was in the depths of depression. Do you know how he found hope? By realizing that God was in charge of the world (Job 42:1-3).

Sometimes we think we deserve better than what we have. We deserve better friends. We deserve more money. We deserve to have the same electronics and expensive toys that others have. When we do not get what we want, we get depressed. Sometimes life does seem unfair. Look at Job. What was fair about his children being killed? What was fair about losing everything he owned? From our perspective, Job's tragedy does not seem fair. However, we can have hope when we approach God as Job eventually did, admitting that God is in control and that, really, we *deserve* nothing (Job 42:4-6). We know that God does love us. We understand that we are part of God's family, and so, although we deserve nothing, we have hope because God is our Father.

The last chapter of Job sums up the rest of Job's life. God honors Job's hope in God's control. In fact, in Job's case, God gave him more wealth and more children. God does not always reward like that, but God knows best how to give each person hope. God does give hope, and we can read about that hope in the Bible.

Handing It Down

Teaching 8: We Should Read the Bible

Review Theme Verse

People do not live by bread alone; rather we live by every word that comes from the mouth of the LORD. (Deuteronomy 8:3b NLT)

Digging Down

The Bible tells us that God wants us to read the Bible publicly, with others (1 Tim. 4:13), but God also wants us to read it by ourselves. This story may help us understand why:

* * *

This morning Alex was running late for school. Usually he woke up fine when his alarm clock went off, but today he rolled over and went back to sleep. So when he got up, he had to rush around, gulp down his breakfast, and throw on clothes, not really caring if they matched. He didn't have time to read even a little of his Bible like he usually did, so as he brushed his teeth, he thought about the verse he read yesterday, "Love your neighbor as yourself" (Mark 12:31). He finished getting ready, and, as his mom handed him his lunch box, he dashed out the door and down the street to meet Chris at the bus stop.

As Alex ran up to their usual meeting spot, he noticed Chris was surrounded by a group of bigger boys. "Uh oh," he thought, "What are those guys saying to Chris?" Alex stopped running, quickly prayed for courage, and then walked up to Chris. Fortunately, the bus pulled up at the same time, and Chris and Alex stepped on.

Their favorite seat, the one in the fourth row on the right side, was not taken, so they slid in and sat down. "What were those boys saying?"

Chris shifted uneasily in his seat, acting a little embarrassed. "They want me to help them play a joke on my neighbor, Sid. It sounds like it might be fun, so I told them I would." After explaining the joke, Chris asked if Alex would help him.

Alex wondered what to say. The joke didn't seem very funny. In fact, it seemed kind of mean. However, he was such good friends with Chris, how could he say no? What harm would just one, small joke do? He definitely didn't want Chris to think that he was not fun. However, the verse he had read in the Bible came back to him.

* * *

Alex was in a quandary. What should he do?

Look Up and Read Psalm 119: 9-16

How can a young person stay on the path of purity? By living according to your word. I seek you with all my heart; do not let me stray from your commands. I have hidden your word in my heart that I might not sin against you. Praise be to you, LORD; teach me your decrees. With my lips I recount all the laws that come from your mouth. I rejoice in following your statutes as one rejoices in great riches. I meditate on your precepts and consider your ways. I delight in your decrees; I will not neglect your word.

What do you think God would want Alex to do? Alex knew that God would want him to be kind because he had read it in the Bible. Verse 11 of what we just read states, "I have hidden your word in my heart that I might not sin against you." God wants each of us to spend time reading the Bible ourselves so God can teach us what he wants us to know. In fact, if we say we are Christians but spend no time learning what that means, then how are we going to make right decisions in situations like the one Alex was faced with? In order to live how God wants us to live, we must read the Bible to know what it says.

Questions

1. What should Alex do? How do you know?

2. What are things we can do so that we learn what the Bible says?

3. Is there a time during the day that you can spend reading the Bible?

DIGGING DEEPER

It is important that we all read the Bible ourselves. Think about your best friend. How much time do you spend being with or talking to that friend? Now consider what your friendship would be like if the only time you talked with that friend was when you were both with a large group of people for an hour a week. What would your friendship be like? And yet, often that is what we do with God. We spend one hour a week reading the Bible with a big group at church, and we expect that to hold us over for the week.

If you are privileged to own a Bible, then you have an amazing opportunity to have a growing, deepening friendship with God. So, where should you start reading?

In most books one would start reading on page one. However, the Bible is arranged a little differently, and so you may not want to start on the first page. The Bible has an Old Testament, which deals with the time before Jesus was on the earth, and a New Testament which deals with the time when Jesus was on earth and after he went back up to heaven. Both the Old Testament and the New Testament are made up of smaller books, which have been loosely categorized in the following table:

Old Testament

History:

Genesis, Exodus, Leviticus, Numbers, Deuteronomy, Joshua, Judges, Ruth, 1 & 2 Samuel, 1 & 2 Kings, 1 & 2 Chronicles, Ezra, Nehemiah, Esther

Writings (poetry, wisdom):

Job, Psalms, Proverbs, Ecclesiastes, Song of Songs

Prophets (written to teach and warn):

Isaiah, Jeremiah, Lamentations, Ezekiel, Daniel, Hosea, Joel, Amos, Obadiah, Jonah, Micah, Nahum, Habakkuk, Zephaniah, Haggai, Zechariah, Malachi

New Testament

Life of Jesus:

Matthew, Mark, Luke, John

History of the Early Church:

Acts

Letters Written by Early Christian Leaders:

Romans, 1 & 2 Corinthians, Galatians, Ephesians, Philippians, Colossians, 1 & 2 Thessalonians, 1 & 2 Timothy, Titus, Philemon, Hebrews, James, 1 & 2 Peter, 1, 2 & 3 John, Jude

Prophecy (written to teach and warn):

Revelation

If you have never read about Jesus' life, then you would probably want to start reading Matthew, Mark, Luke, or John. If you enjoy history, then perhaps Genesis or Acts would be a good place to begin. It does not matter where you start; the important thing is to spend time reading the Bible for yourself.

SECTION 2

DOCTRINE OF GOD

OVERVIEW

Where did our world come from? Who established the law of gravity and other laws of our universe? Is it coincidence that brings so many "chance" events into our lives? Why do people seem determined to have some sort of religion, whether it is Buddhism, Islam, Atheism, Christianity, or something else? Why are we on this earth?

Do you ever think about these questions? Most of us ponder questions like these at some point in our lives. As Christians, our answers differ from those of other religions. We believe that *God* is the creator of the universe, that *God* is the power behind the universe continuing to exist and function, and that the reason why people are on this earth is so they can glorify God.

What does it mean to glorify God? One meaning is to build God's reputation, or to spread God's fame.¹ Everything was created to build God's reputation: to glorify God. In this section your family will examine some of God's attributes. By learning about these attributes, your children's understanding of God will increase and thus God's reputation will increase. Your children will also learn about some of God's actions, such as planning salvation and revealing himself to us. As your children increase in knowledge, they will have a greater awe and appreciation for what God has done. Again, God is glorified because his reputation has grown. What a wonderful opportunity you have to help your children understand a bit about God and thus glorify him.

Our theme verse for the Doctrine of God includes all of that information.

For from him: Everything, including all of creation, comes from God.

And through him: The universe, including people, continues to exist and function because of God's intervention and planning.

And for him are all things: All things exist for God.

To him be the glory forever! Amen: Everything comes from God, survives through his power, and exists to make God famous and to build his reputation.

What a verse showing us God's power, wisdom, creativity, and purpose for people! You will have the chance to memorize this verse as you learn about the doctrine of God.

Theme Verse for Memorization: Romans 11:36

For from him and through him and for him are all things. To him be the glory forever! Amen.

Let's learn who God is.

Teaching 1: The Trinity

Review Theme Verse

For from him and through him and for him are all things. To him be the glory forever! Amen. (Romans 11:36)

Digging Down

If you have an extra egg in your kitchen, crack it open into a bowl. What are the three parts you see? (If you do not have an egg, just describe the three parts). There is the hard shell, the clear (or white) part, and the yellow yolk. Three different parts make up one egg. Each part is different, but in order to have the complete egg, you must have all three parts. This illustration is often used to try to describe the Trinity. Just like the one egg has three parts, there are also three persons in our one God: God the Father, Jesus the Son, and the Holy Spirit. Three separate persons are part of our one God. This is called the Trinity: three in one.

We can compare the Trinity of God to an egg, and there are some similarities because both the egg and the Trinity have three parts that make up one whole. However, we must understand that the Trinity is much more than an egg! For instance, the shell of an egg is just the shell; it is not the complete egg. The yolk is just the yolk; it is not the complete egg. However, God the Father is completely God, Jesus the Son is completely God, and the Holy Spirit is completely God. They do not need each other to be completely whole, and yet together they make one whole. Isn't that amazing? God exists as three complete, equal persons but is one whole. How does this work? We cannot fully explain it, and we cannot even fully understand it, but we see the Trinity in the Bible, and so we know that it is true.

Look Up and Read Matthew 3:16-17

As soon as Jesus was baptized, he went up out of the water. At that moment heaven was opened, and he saw the Spirit of God descending like a dove and alighting on him. And a voice from heaven said, "This is my Son, whom I love; with him I am well pleased."

Right after Jesus was baptized, an extraordinary event showed those present all three separate persons of the Trinity: God the Father, Jesus the Son, and the Holy Spirit. Jesus the Son was the one standing in the water being baptized. Then, the Holy Spirit came down, looking like a dove, and rested on Jesus. God the Father stated, "This is my Son, whom I love; with him I am well pleased." In these verses we see that all three exist separately at the same time, and yet all three are God together.

The Trinity is hard for us to understand, but the Bible tells about it so we know it is true! To summarize, if someone asks you what the Trinity is, you could state that we believe in One God who is made up of three persons: God the Father, Jesus the Son, and the Holy Spirit. The Trinity means three persons in one God.

Questions

1. What does Trinity mean?

2. What is one event in the Bible when we read about all three parts of the Trinity?

3. How is the Trinity similar to an egg? How is it different?

4. We cannot fully understand the Trinity, so why do we believe it is true?

Digging Deeper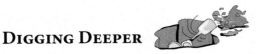

We believe that there are three persons, God the Father, Jesus the Son, and the Holy Spirit, who make up our one God. This is called the Trinity. All three of these persons have existed forever and will continue to exist forever. All three are completely God.

There are some people, however, who believe that all three are God, but do not believe that they all exist at the same time. These people believe that God the Father is the one who created the universe and earth, and God the Father is also the God whom we read about in the Old Testament. Then, God stopped being God the Father when he became Jesus the Son and lived on this earth two thousand years ago. After Jesus the Son died and rose again, God then changed to become the Holy Spirit who lives in all Christians now. In other words, these people believe that the one God was not made up of three persons, but rather changed form three times. This is called Modalism. God changed his form, or "mode," three times. However, Christians do not believe this because the Bible teaches that all three exist at the same time.

We read in Matthew 3 about Jesus' baptism. There we saw the simultaneous existence of all three persons of God: God the Father, Jesus the Son, and the Holy Spirit. There are other places where we read that all three persons of the Trinity exist at the same time. One of these verses is 2 Corinthians 13:14, "May the grace of the Lord Jesus Christ, and the love of God, and the fellowship of the Holy Spirit be with you all."

Here, Paul ended his letter by referring to the grace that Jesus Christ gives, the love that God the Father gives, and the fellowship that the Holy Spirit gives. All three of these persons had something to give to those who lived in Corinth. Thus, all three must exist at the same time.

There are many difficult ideas, such as the Trinity, that are taught in the Bible. When we are faced with these difficult ideas, we have a choice. We can either decide that the Bible is untrue, or we can have faith that it is true even if we cannot understand it all. As people we sometimes think that we should be able to figure everything out, and thus it is difficult to believe in something we do not understand. However, it should not be difficult to believe that the creator of the universe, the being who knows everything, and the power behind our lives is beyond our understanding! The more we learn about God, the more our amazement will grow.

The Bible tells us that God is one God with three equal, complete persons: God the Father, Jesus the Son, and the Holy Spirit. Although we cannot fully understand it, we have faith that it is true.

Teaching 2: God Is Sovereign

Review Theme Verse

For from him and through him and for him are all things. To him be the glory forever! Amen. (Romans 11:36)

DIGGING DOWN

Who is someone who has authority over you? You might name a parent, police officer, teacher, or boss. If you do something wrong, what does that authority do to you? Everyone on earth has someone who is in authority over him or her. Even the most powerful person on earth has God as an authority over them.

In the Bible we read about God's sovereignty, or his authority, over Nebuchadnezzar, a very powerful king in the ancient realm of Babylon. King Nebuchadnezzar led armies to conquer many nations. He was incredibly rich and had huge palaces with everything he wanted. In fact, he was the king who ordered the construction of the *Hanging Gardens of Babylon*, one of the "Seven Wonders of the Ancient World."[2] This is also the King who demanded that everyone bow down to a huge statue he made of himself, and then he threw Shadrach, Meshach, and Abednego into a fiery furnace because they refused to do so (Dan. 3). This king was the authority over a huge number of people. However, even the ruler Nebuchadnezzar had an authority, or ruler, over him. Who was the ruler over Nebuchadnezzar? God. God was the Super-Ruler over Nebuchadnezzar just as God is the Super-Ruler, or sovereign, over every person and every thing.

In the book of Daniel, we read of when King Nebuchadnezzar was proud about how powerful he was. However, God wanted even King Nebuchadnezzar to realize that no one on earth has as much authority or sovereignty as God does. One time, when Nebuchadnezzar was bragging about his power, God told him that he would become like a wild animal. Nebuchadnezzar would then live like a wild animal until he admitted that God is sovereign and in control. Nebuchadnezzar probably doubted that God could actually do anything to him. However, God did exactly what he said he would do.

Look Up and Read Daniel 4:33-35

Immediately what had been said about Nebuchadnezzar was fulfilled. He was driven away from people and ate grass like the ox. His body was drenched with the dew of heaven until his hair grew like the feathers of an eagle and his nails like the claws of a bird. At the end of that time, I, Nebuchadnezzar, raised my eyes toward heaven, and my sanity was restored. Then I praised the Most High; I honored and glorified him who lives forever. His dominion is an eternal dominion; his kingdom endures from generation to generation. All the peoples of the earth are regarded as nothing. He does as he pleases with the powers of heaven and the peoples of the earth. No one can hold back his hand or say to him: "What have you done?"

King Nebuchadnezzar needed to learn that, no matter how much authority or control one has, God has even more. God is sovereign.

God is the Super-Ruler. One translation of the Bible, the NET Bible, translates verse 35 as, "No one slaps God's hand and says to him, 'What have you done?'"³ Because we do not have control over God, we do not have the right to demand anything from God. Probably none of us will have to live like a wild animal so that we understand that God is sovereign, but it is still a lesson that we all must learn.

God is sovereign. God is the authority. We need to understand that, just as a parent has authority over a child or a teacher has authority over those in the classroom, God has authority over everything on earth. No one tells him what to do. No one slaps his hand.

Questions

1. What is another word we could use for "sovereign"?

2. What happened to King Nebuchadnezzar so that he knew that God had authority over everything and everyone?

3. How did Nebuchadnezzar respond to God causing him to live like a wild animal?

4. Who is sovereign over everything and everyone?

Digging Deeper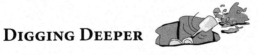

The Merriam-Webster dictionary defines one who is sovereign as "one who exercises supreme authority within a limited sphere."⁴ King Nebuchadnezzar fits that definition. Nebuchadnezzar was sovereign, or in authority, over just his kingdom, not over every land mass or every human in the entire world. King Nebuchadnezzar's sovereignty was a limited sovereignty. However, when we talk about God's sovereignty, we say that his authority is limitless. Nothing in the entire universe lies outside the sphere of his authority. We see this theme of God's sovereignty throughout the Bible.

Look Up and Read 1 Timothy 6:13-16

In the sight of God, who gives life to everything, and of Christ Jesus, who while testifying before Pontius Pilate made the good confession, I charge you to keep this command without spot or blame until the appearing of our Lord Jesus Christ, which God will bring about in his own time—God, the blessed and only Ruler, the King of kings and Lord of lords, who alone is immortal and who lives in unapproachable light, whom no one has seen or can see. To him be honor and might forever. Amen.

These verses state that God gives life to everything; God is sovereign; God is the King above all kings and the Lord above all other lords. God possesses immortality; God has eternal power. All of these descriptions show us that God is sovereign and in authority over every person and thing.

Of course, many people in this world do not want to acknowledge God's sovereignty. By their actions they try to prove that they are sovereign over themselves. Because people want to prove they have control over their looks, they buy expensive make-up, have plastic surgery to change their nose or remove wrinkles, and lift weights to boost muscle mass. But what happens? They continue to age, wrinkles come back, an unsightly mole appears, and who has seen an eighty year old with huge muscles? We may fight hard to control our looks, but we cannot actually achieve sovereignty over them.

Some people say they will have sovereignty or authority in their career. They work hard, graduate with a Doctorate degree, or achieve the highest office in their business. However, eventually someone else replaces them. Or perhaps a natural disaster destroys the business; maybe even a financial crisis rocks the nation or world. People are not sovereign in the business world.

Some people even try to achieve sovereignty over their nation. History records how ruler after ruler rises to power just to have it wrested away as another ambitious person overthrows the one in power. In fact, even in the short time that a ruler is powerful, it is a limited power just as Nebuchadnezzar's was. The ruler's power lies only within the time and space of the ruler; it does not cover all time and the entire universe.

Impressively, God's sovereignty is not limited to a specific sphere. God has sovereignty that is not shaken by the world financial market, aging, or national boundaries. God's authority spans all time, all space, and all circumstances. Ultimately, God alone is sovereign.

Teaching 3: God Is Holy

Review Theme Verse

> For from him and through him and for him are all things. To him be the glory forever! Amen. (Romans 11:36)

Digging Down

What type of dishes did you use at the last meal you ate? Are these the dishes that you usually use? Now think of other dishes your family may have. Does your family own any that are saved for special occasions? Perhaps there is a whole set of dishes that you use only when company comes. Or perhaps your family owns a beautiful bowl that you never use because it is so special. It is set apart because it is a special, unique bowl. Perhaps you do not own any set-apart dishes, but you do own a toy or book that you do not want others to use because it is so special to you. In fact, it may be so special that you do not even play with it often! We all may have special dishes, toys, or books that we decide not to use every day. They are set apart because they are unique or meaningful to us. Understanding our set apart dishes, toys, or books will help us understand a bit about God.

God is holy. Holy means to be "set apart from that which is commonplace, [to be] special, [to be] unique."[5] God is set apart from everything commonplace because he is more special and unique than anything we know. God is holy.

Throughout the Bible there are many references to God being more special, better, and different from anything we know. God is holy. Let's look at some verses that describe a scene in heaven.

Look Up and Read Revelation 4:6-8

Also in front of the throne there was what looked like a sea of glass, clear as crystal. In the center, around the throne, were four living creatures, and they were covered with eyes, in front and in back. The first living creature was like a lion, the second was like an ox, the third had a face like a man, the fourth was like a flying eagle. Each of the four living creatures had six wings and was covered with eyes all around, even under its wings. Day and night they never stop saying: "'Holy, holy, holy is the Lord God Almighty,' who was, and is, and is to come."

In these verses we read of living creatures with six wings and who are covered in eyes. They are surrounding the throne of God continually saying, "Holy, holy, holy is the Lord God Almighty, who was and is, and is to come" (v. 8b). God is holy. God is set apart and special. Even these creatures that appear very odd to us recognize that God is above, beyond, and set apart from everything else.

You will also notice that they don't just say that God is holy once. They repeat it three times, emphasizing God's holiness.[6] So, God is not only one holy. Nor is he as amazing as two holies. No, to describe

God they had to say it three times. "Holy, holy, holy." Wow, God is so set apart and special that they repeated it three times!

This verse also tells us why these creatures are calling God special, set apart, holy. They say God is the one "who was, and is, and is to come" (v. 8b). God is eternal. God is set apart from all the rest of creation because he never began, he exists today, and he will never end. God is special. God is holy.

Questions

1. What does "holy" mean?

2. When a word is repeated in the Bible (like holy, holy, holy), what does that tell us?

3. In Revelation 4:8, the living creatures say that God is holy, set apart, for a specific reason. What is the reason that they state?

4. What are some other ways that God is holy, set apart?

Digging Deeper

Isaiah was a prophet in the Old Testament who had the unique experience of getting a brief glimpse into heaven. Let's find out what Isaiah saw.

Look Up and Read Isaiah 6:1-5

> In the year that King Uzziah died, I saw the Lord, high and exalted, seated on a throne; and the train of his robe filled the temple. Above him were seraphim, each with six wings: With two wings they covered their faces, with two they covered their feet, and with two they were flying. And they were calling to one another: "Holy, holy, holy is the LORD Almighty; the whole earth is full of his glory." At the sound of their voices the doorposts and thresholds shook and the temple was filled with smoke. "Woe to me!" I cried. "I am ruined!

For I am a man of unclean lips, and I live among a people of unclean lips, and my eyes have seen the King, the LORD Almighty."

Isaiah saw God seated on a throne and around the throne were flying seraphim loudly proclaiming the holiness of God. Interestingly, these seraphim said exactly what the creatures in Revelation 4:8 said. They repeated the description, "Holy," three times. "Holy, holy, holy." God's level of holiness is not just one or two "holies," but he is at the top: three "holies."

The writer of this passage emphasized two ways in which God is holy, set apart, above people. The first is found in verse one. We read that the hem of God's robe fills the temple. God is so large that not even his whole robe fits into a huge building. Only the hem fits in! God is holy, set apart, and unique in his creation because he is different from it. God is also described as a King and the Lord Almighty (or the Lord who leads armies). Because God is the king above all other kings and more powerful than anything else in all creation, God is set apart. God is holy.

> He is the God who spoke the universe into being, and so ours is a God of omnipotent power and creative order. He is the God who summoned Abraham to a pilgrimage of faith and appeared to him at least nine times, so He is a personal God who addresses His people individually. Our God gave Moses His divine law in the ethereal reaches of Sinai, so He is a God who not only protects but also makes moral demands on His people in accordance with His own character. Through Amos, He rebuked His chosen people (and us today) with stern promises of judgment for the wanton disregard of his moral law; through Hosea He assured them (and us) of His unrelenting love. This God repeatedly tells His people, "I am holy."
> - *Donald N. Bastian*[7]

In these verses we also read of God's set-apartness by his moral uniqueness. After Isaiah saw the awesomeness of God, he understood his own sinfulness. Verse five shows that Isaiah recognized that his lips were so sinful they could not praise this holy, awesome God. Realizing that he had used his mouth and words to sin, Isaiah felt that he could not use that same mouth to talk about this holy, set apart, special God. And Isaiah was only lamenting the sinfulness of his mouth! He did not even get to the sinfulness of the rest of him. Think of all the sin that we do with our mind, our mouths, and our bodies. We are different than God. We are sinful. God is holy; he is set apart because God has never sinned.

God is set apart. God is different than anything in all of creation. God is unique. God is holy.

Teaching 4: God Is Jealous

Review Theme Verse

For from him and through him and for him are all things. To him be the glory forever! Amen. (Romans 11:36)

Digging Down

Let's read a story about Emily's new bike.

* * *

"Yahoo! I wanted a new bike. Thanks, Mom and Dad, for my birthday bike!" Emily got on her new purple bicycle and rode down the quiet street, giving her teddy bear, Frosty, a ride in the basket. She rode her bike all afternoon and didn't stop until it was time to go inside for dinner and birthday cake. That night, as she was lying in bed, she remembered that she left Frosty in the bike basket. "Oh well," she thought, "Frosty can go with me to Liza's house tomorrow when I ride my bike over to play."

The next morning after breakfast Emily rushed out to the garage, grabbed her helmet, and looked at where she had left her bike. It was gone! She searched all over the garage. Her bike was not there. She looked around her yard, wondering if perhaps her younger brother had put it somewhere. But her bike was nowhere to be found.

"I'm sorry, Emily," her mom said. "I'll drive you to Liza's house and we can look for your bike later."

Emily climbed into the backseat of the car. On the way through town, she noticed a girl riding a beautiful purple bike. "Oh, she looks like she is having so much fun—just like I did on my bike." Emily felt jealousy welling up inside her heart. Then she sat bolt upright. What was that on the front of the girl's bike? It was a bear sitting in the basket. The bear looked a lot like Frosty.

"Mom, I think that girl has my bike!" Emily cried out as they passed the girl. Her mom quickly stopped the car and asked about the bike, but the girl adamantly claimed that the bike was hers. Emily got so mad because it was obvious that this bike, including the white bear snuggled in the basket, belonged to her, but the girl would not give it to her. Emily was furious! This was her bike, and she wanted it back!

* * *

Was Emily right in wanting her bike back? Was she right to get angry about it? If the girl did not give the bike back, is it right for Emily to be jealous of the girl riding her bike? Often we are jealous when we want something that is not ours, and that is a wrong time to be jealous. However, jealousy is a right emotion to have if we are jealous because we want something that is rightfully ours.

Look Up and Read Exodus 20:4-6

You shall not make for yourself an image in the form of anything in heaven above or on the earth beneath or in the waters below. You shall not bow down to them or worship them; for I, the LORD your God, am a jealous God, punishing the children for the sin of the parents to the third and fourth generation of those who hate me, but showing love to a thousand generations of those who love me and keep my commandments.

Here is one of the Ten Commandments, and it says that we should not make any idols nor should we worship anything or anyone besides God. Why? Because all worship belongs to God. Then verse five says that God is a jealous God, and if we do worship anything or anyone besides him, then he will punish us. Worship belongs to God, and when we give it to someone or something else, then God has the right emotion of jealousy.

All worship belongs to God. Nothing else deserves people's worship and dedication. And yet, people often give their worship and dedication to something or someone besides God. Just as Emily got jealous when she saw the girl riding her stolen bike, so God gets jealous when someone takes the worship that belongs to him and gives it to someone or something else.

Questions

1. Was Emily right in being jealous that the other girl had her bike? Why?

2. When is it not right to be jealous?

3. Why does God get jealous?

4. Why is it right for God to get jealous about our worship?

Digging Deeper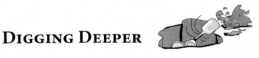

Many times in the Bible God talks about being a jealous God. God demands all of our worship and dedication, and yet we often find other people or things to worship. Think about it for a minute. What do you spend most of your time doing? What is something or someone you would really miss if it was taken away from you? Now think about whether this thing or person is more important to you than learning about God or serving him. If it is, then you may be worshipping this other thing or person more than you are worshipping God. It is not wrong to have hobbies or to love others. However, we must be very careful that we do not put those things or people above God.

Look Up and Read Nahum 1:2-4

> *The LORD is a jealous and avenging God; the LORD takes vengeance and is filled with wrath. The LORD takes vengeance on his foes and vents his wrath against his enemies. The LORD is slow to anger but great in power; the LORD will not leave the guilty unpunished. His way is in the whirlwind and the storm, and clouds are the dust of his feet. He rebukes the sea and dries it up; he makes all the rivers run dry. Bashan and Carmel wither and the blossoms of Lebanon fade.*

God is jealous. God is vengeful. We sometimes do not like to think about those attributes of God. We like to think about other attributes, such as how he is slow to anger and great in power (Nah. 1:3), or how God is "good, a refuge in times of trouble" (Nah. 1:7). However, God is also jealous when we give our worship, which belongs to him, to someone or something else.

In fact, Exodus 34:14 says, "Do not worship any other god, for the LORD, whose name is Jealous, is a jealous God." God's character is so full of jealousy for the worship that belongs to him, that one of his names is "Jealous!"

The Old Testament is full of warnings that people should only worship God or they would be punished. Because they did not heed those warnings, God destroyed their land. Do we take God seriously in only worshipping him?

The idea that God is a jealous God who will punish those who turn from him is not just found in the Old Testament. In 1 Corinthians

10:18-22, Paul wrote a warning to those in Corinth to make sure that they truly gave all their worship to God because, if they didn't, then they would stir up God's jealousy. If we don't want to stir up God's jealousy (and we definitely do not!), then we should be very aware that we must worship only God.

Teaching 5: God Is Eternal

Review Theme Verse

For from him and through him and for him are all things. To him be the glory forever! Amen. (Romans 11:36)

Digging Down

"I am hungry." Have you ever said that? What does that mean? It means that, at the very moment you said it, you were hungry. It does not mean that you were hungry in the past or that you will be hungry in the future, but that you are hungry right now. Have you ever said, "I am tired?" Again, that does not mean that you wanted a nap yesterday, nor does it say that tomorrow you will want a nap. No, "I am tired" means that right now, at this very moment, you are tired.

We all live just in this present moment. We all have a past (what happened last year or yesterday) and a future (what will happen later today or next year), but what we live right now, at this very moment, is the present. So, when you say, "I am thirsty," you are saying that in the present you would like a drink.

People have a past and a future, but God does not because God is eternal. God never began and will never die. God has lived forever and will continue to live forever. In fact, when God told Moses to convince the Israelites that God will free them, God gives himself a name that shows that he always lives in the present and that he does not have a beginning or an end.

Look Up and Read Exodus 3:13-14

> *Moses said to God, "Suppose I go to the Israelites and say to them, 'The God of your fathers has sent me to you,' and they ask me, 'What is his name?' Then what shall I tell them?" God said to Moses, "I AM WHO I AM. This is what you are to say to the Israelites: 'I AM has sent me to you.'"*

What was the name that God called himself? "I Am." This name showed Moses and the Israelites that God always existed and will always exist because "I Am" is in the present. Without beginning or end, God is "I Am."

Because we all have a beginning point and our bodies will have an end when we die, it is hard for us to understand that God never began and will never end. To help us understand, let's think about God's power. Before the earth was created, God could say, "I am powerful." When Moses was living, God could say, "I am powerful." Again, God is talking in the present, "I am." Today, God could say, "I am powerful," and three hundred years from now God could say, "I am powerful." In fact, God will never stop saying, "I am powerful." Power is just one attribute of God, but because God can say "I am" at every moment of time shows that God is eternal.

Questions

1. What is one statement that you can make that shows something about yourself right now in the present (e.g. "I am hungry.")?

2. What is the name that God gives himself in Exodus 3:14?

3. When God names himself "I Am," what do we learn about God?

Digging Deeper

Have you ever seen a movie or television show that is about a person traveling through time? Some have the main character traveling backwards and meeting himself or his ancestors. Others have the hero or heroine traveling forward to witness future events. Although we know that we live in the present, we are very aware that there have been generations who have lived and struggled before us and there will be generations that will exist after our bodies have been buried. We view time as a line, and each person's life is a part of the timeline through human history. The large selection of television shows or movies based on time-travel show that people are fascinated with the idea of time. There is another dimension of time that most movies do not talk about but that is equally as fascinating to ponder.

Look Up and Read Psalm 90:1-4

Lord, you have been our dwelling place throughout all generations. Before the mountains were born or you brought forth the whole world, from everlasting to everlasting you are God. You turn people back to dust, saying, "Return to dust, you mortals." A thousand years in your sight are like a day that has just gone by, or like a watch in the night.

These verses show us that God is not bound by time as people are bound by time. God existed before the mountains or the earth. God has been God and will be God "from everlasting to everlasting" (v. 2). In other words, God has no beginning and end, just like we read about earlier. However, these verses say even more about God's eternality. Verse four states that, to God, one thousand years is like a day or even like the shortness of a night. Because God is eternal, because he has no beginning or end, God does not live within time. God exists outside of the human timeline. God is eternal.

This means that God is listening to your prayers and interacting with your life at the same time that he told Moses that his name was "I Am." God sees your great-grandfather while watching your own grandchildren play. God is eternal and is not bound by our time. God sees King David, the Apostle Paul, and us in the same glance. That is an amazing God. That is a God worth listening to because, although our view is narrowed by our own point on the timeline, God's view is not. God's view is eternal, and God is not limited by the present on a human timeline.

Family Fun

Try one or more of these with your family to help you explain that God sees us when we are children, and he knows us when we are adults. This should be a comforting time as you assure your children that God will continue to take care of them in their future because he will be there just as he has been in their past.

1. Get out pictures or videos of your children when they were smaller. Enjoy looking at them together and telling your children stories about when they were younger. Even young children enjoy hearing about when they were babies! Include some stories of when God provided for your family, or when he gave a special experience to you. If you have pictures of you or your ancestors, look at those and tell of how God provided in your family history. Assure your children that God will be in their future, just as he has been in the past!

2. Take time as a family to dream. Is there a special trip that you would like to take or some way you would like to help someone? As you dream about your future, let your children give ideas as well. Then spend some time praying about those dreams as a

family. With the knowledge that God does exist in the future, you can ask him to help your family accomplish the goals that he wants you to accomplish.

Teaching 6: God: Revealed Through General Revelation

Review Theme Verse

For from him and through him and for him are all things. To him be the glory forever! Amen. (Romans 11:36)

Digging Down

How would you describe God? Try to have every person in your group come up with a different description of God. These descriptions, such as powerful, creative, and wise, are called attributes of God. The Bible reveals to us or teaches us about many attributes of God, including those that you mentioned. When God reveals something about himself through the Bible, it is called Special Revelation. Because "revelation" means "to reveal," Special Revelation means that God revealed information through a special, specific source – the Bible. However, did you know that the Bible is not the only place where we can learn about God?

Look Up and Read Romans 1:18-20

The wrath of God is being revealed from heaven against all the godlessness and wickedness of people, who suppress the truth by their wickedness, since what may be known about God is plain to them, because God has made it plain to them. For since the creation of the world God's invisible qualities—his eternal power and divine nature—have been clearly seen, being understood from what has been made, so that people are without excuse.

These verses state there is another place where God reveals information about himself. Where is that? We can learn about God in what has been made. In other words, we can learn about God from looking at creation, including the world around us.

For example, think about how a tree grows. A small seed must be buried, and then just the right amount of sunlight and water must hit the seed. After a time, roots grow down and the sprout grows up. Below ground, the roots soak up the necessary nutrients and become a strong support for the growing tree. Above ground, bark, oxygen-producing leaves, and possibly fruit grow. It then produces a seed that is ready to generate another tree. In order to be successful, the entire process from seed to enormous tree requires specific conditions.

Think about what would happen if the process of a tree growing was not such a well-ordered progression. Roots would be growing up instead of down; apples might grow on the roots of a mango tree, and leaves might stop producing the oxygen we need to breathe. However, this planet is covered with well-ordered trees from which we can expect oxygen and fruit. And this is only a tree! Think of how well ordered all the rest of creation is. Why is it that way? Because the God who created it shows his eternal power and divine nature by knowing exactly how to create a universe that will work.

Romans 1:20 says that we see God's eternal power from creation. One way that we see his power in the development of a tree is that one tree produces more trees. This process of tree producing tree will continue until God stops it. God has the power throughout all time to continue the processes that are in his creation.

Romans 1:20 also says that we can learn about God's divine nature from examining creation. God is divine, which means that God is in

Handing It Down

control. God controls all of nature, and because we see nature we can see how God controls it.

When God reveals something about himself in creation, we call that General Revelation. The next time you are taking a walk, watching people, or learning about nature, think about how creation teaches us about God by giving us General Revelation.

Questions

1. What is Special Revelation?
2. What is General Revelation?
3. What can we learn about God by looking at his creation?

Digging Deeper

Imagine you are going on a walk. At one point, you notice that you almost stepped on a watch.[8] You pick it up to examine it. It has a black plastic band; the numbers glow green on the silver-grey background. You notice that it is a relatively simple watch because it has no features such as a stop-watch. How did this simple timepiece get in your path?

Perhaps the wind, grass, and a worm all mixed together at exactly the right moment and in the exact proportions to create this watch! This is a simple watch, after all, so perhaps it could have come about by chance. Doesn't this sound ridiculous? Saying that a watch, no matter how simple, could be created by chance elements combining, even if given billions of years, is preposterous. We understand that something as complex as a simple watch would need to have a creator behind it.

When we accept the idea that watches, shoes, earrings, and even combs all have creators, then why is it so difficult to accept that trees, flowers, and the sun also have a creator? In fact, trees, flowers, and the sun are much more complex then a simple watch, so it seems that if a simple thing such as a watch needs a creator, then surely a complex item would have one! And yet, for some reason, people refuse to believe in a God that created the universe.

Look Up and Read Romans 1:20-22

> For since the creation of the world God's invisible qualities—his eternal power and divine nature—have been clearly seen, being understood from what has been made, so that people are without excuse. For although they knew God, they neither glorified him as God nor gave thanks to him, but their thinking became futile and their foolish hearts were darkened. Although they claimed to be wise, they became fools.

What do these verses show us about those who deny a creator God? They are fools, even though they claim to be wise. So much evidence points to a creator who is wise, orderly, and beyond our time and space. And yet some people refuse to acknowledge that our existence points to a creator. Perhaps their refusal stems from their desire for independence. If there is a creator, then someone or something has the right to control their lives. Whatever the reason, the Bible makes it clear that to ignore the evidence pointing to a creator is not wise.

As you study our existence, from the miniscule building blocks of matter to the massive galaxies beyond our galaxy, be amazed at the creativity, orderliness, size, and beauty of it all. Be amazed and remember its Creator.

Teaching 7: God Planned Salvation

Review Theme Verse

For from him and through him and for him are all things. To him be the glory forever! Amen. (Romans 11:36)

DIGGING DOWN

Have you ever helped to plan a party, perhaps at your birthday, New Year's, or some other holiday that you celebrate? What are the things you would need to plan? Probably you would think about where to have the gathering, what to eat, and what activities everyone who comes could do together. You would even need to plan who you are going to invite. Long before the day of the party, you would spend time thinking about and planning the event because most big events take quite a bit of planning!

As Christians, we believe that there was a big event that happened about two thousand years ago that impacted our lives. Do you know what that event was? Two thousand years ago Jesus died on the cross and rose again in order to glorify God and give us salvation. That is a big event that impacts us!

However, as we said, every big event takes planning, and Jesus dying for our salvation is no exception. In fact, the Bible tells us that God the Father planned Jesus' death and resurrection before the earth was even created!

Look Up and Read Ephesians 1:4-5

For he chose us in him before the creation of the world to be holy and blameless in his sight. In love, he predestined us for adoption to sonship through Jesus Christ, in accordance with his pleasure and will.

Before God created the world, he planned to adopt us into his family through Jesus' death and resurrection. Imagine that! Just as you plan a party and decide who to invite, so God planned the event of salvation, and he chose to invite you! Wow. You have been invited by the creator of the universe to be adopted into his family. That should make you feel pretty special!

It was not an accident that Jesus was born in Bethlehem two thousand years ago. God chose the exact right place and time for his event of salvation to happen. And it was not a surprise to God that Jesus was crucified. It also was not a surprise that Jesus did not stay dead, but that he rose again and then went up to heaven to live. God planned the whole event so that we could be adopted into his family, and so that we could be holy and blameless in his sight.

If you ever doubt God's love for you, remember that God planned to invite you into his family long before he created trees, birds, or even lakes. God planned for salvation, and God chose you. Now you need to decide if you are going to accept his invitation.

Questions

1. Who planned salvation?

2. What was the event that brought about salvation?

3. What is one reason why God planned salvation?

Digging Deeper

Often when we do something we have more than one motive for doing it. For instance, we may be kind to someone because we actually want to help that person, but we also may want to be known by others as a kind person. Thus, we have two motives for doing that kind action. When God planned salvation, he also had two motives. Look for God's motives in the following scripture.

Look Up and Read Ephesians 2:4-7

> *But because of his great love for us, God, who is rich in mercy, made us alive with Christ even when we were dead in transgressions—it is by grace you have been saved. And God raised us up with Christ and seated us with him in the heavenly realms in Christ Jesus, in order that in the coming ages he might show the incomparable riches of his grace, expressed in his kindness to us in Christ Jesus.*

Did you notice the two motives? The first is in verse four. God has such great love for us that he gives us grace and saves us. Grace is something we are given that we do not deserve. We do not deserve salvation; we can do nothing to earn salvation. However, because of his immense love for us, God gives us undeserved salvation. Because we do not deserve that gift, it is grace.

The second motive of God for planning salvation is in verse seven. God saves us so that, throughout all of eternity, he can show how kind he was when he gave us our undeserved salvation. Can you see the scene in heaven? God points to you and says, "Do you see that person? That person was a sinner! A wretched, evil, selfish sinner. There was absolutely no way that person could have been here in heaven, except…I planned a way for salvation. I planned a special, completely undeserved gift for that person." One of God's motives for planning salvation was so that we could understand more of how kind, generous, and loving he is. In other words, he planned salvation so that we would worship him.

This could be a bit confusing. We usually think that if people do something so that others would praise them, then they are doing it because of their own pride. We also say pride is a sin. Does God sin when he wants us to praise him? Absolutely not. God cannot sin.

It is natural that God would want us to praise him because he is the best, the brightest, the wisest, and the most powerful being. For God to be humble, to think he is less than someone else, would actually be a lie because there is nothing greater than he is. We see his greatness as we think about his plan of salvation.

God planned salvation because of his love for us. God also planned it so that we would worship him for his kindness towards us. As we think about salvation, it is important that we recognize both of God's motives. Only then will we truly worship God as we praise him for his kindness and love in planning salvation.

Teaching 8: God Is Love

Review Theme Verse

For from him and through him and for him are all things. To him be the glory forever! Amen. (Romans 11:36)

DIGGING DOWN

Think of one person who loves you. How do you know that he or she loves you? Take a moment to share who it is and how you know that you are loved by that person.

You might feel love if you received a gift from the person, if you feel that you can always talk with that person, if you can depend on that person, or if you feel safe with that person. Perhaps you came up with different ways that you feel loved, but we probably have all felt loved by a person. Did you know that God also loves us? In fact, God's love is deeper, stronger, and better than any love that we get from a person! That is some kind of love!

Look Up and Read 1 John 4:9-10

> *This is how God showed his love among us: He sent his one and only Son into the world that we might live through him. This is love: not that we loved God, but that he loved us and sent his Son as an atoning sacrifice for our sins.*

These verses talk of a huge way that God showed his love for us. What is it? God sent his only Son into the world. We know that Jesus did not come into the world because of how awesome people are. We know people are not all that awesome – look at the sin we commit! No, Jesus came into the world not because of how amazing people are, but because God is love.

Jesus showed his love by becoming a man and paying for the sin that we commit. God loved us so much that he wanted Jesus to leave heaven, live as a God-man on earth, and then die a horrible, painful death in order to forgive our sins. God loves us that much.

Earlier we mentioned that one way we might know that someone loves us is if that person gives us gifts. Well, we see that God gives us gifts too. In fact, God giving Jesus to us is the most amazing gift that anyone could give us. John 3:16 says, "For God so loved the world that he gave his one and only Son, that whoever believes in him shall not perish but have eternal life." God gave us the gift of Jesus.

As we said before, giving gifts is not the only way that we know that someone loves us. Sometimes we feel love because someone defends us or because we can talk with that person. Did you know that God loves us in those ways as well? The Bible, especially the book of Psalms, is full of assurances that God does defend us, and we know that God listens to us as we pray to him.

Think about all the blessings in our own lives (even the blessing of having people love us!). God allowed all of those blessings to be in our lives because he loves us. God is a faithful, loving God who will never leave us alone to struggle by ourselves. We can depend on God's deep, never-ending love for us.

Questions

1. What is one way that we feel love from another person?

2. How did Jesus' coming into the world show us God's love for us?

3. What are other ways that God shows his love for us?

Digging Deeper

Have you ever seen a spoiled child? How would you describe that child? We have probably all seen children who demand to get whatever they want, and if they do not get it, then they cry, pout, or threaten. As a parent, it would be so easy to just give a child everything he or she wants in order to keep peace! However, if a parent always gives in to the child's demands, then the child grows up without knowing how to love others, how to help others, and how to have self-discipline. In other words, if a child is spoiled by his parents, then the child will not grow into a mature adult who is able to look beyond his or her own needs. So it seems that, if a parent truly loved the child, then the parent would discipline the child so that the child would learn respect, self-discipline, and how to love others. That makes sense in a human family, and yet so often we do not want that same principle to apply to our spiritual family.

In the Bible, God is often referred to as our parent. God loves us, provides for us, and protects us as a responsible parent would. God also disciplines us just as a parent should.

Look Up and Read Hebrews 12:5-9

> *And have you completely forgotten this word of encouragement that addresses you as a father addresses his son? It says, "My son, do not make light of the Lord's discipline, and do not lose heart when he rebukes you, because the Lord disciplines the one he loves, and he chastens everyone he accepts as his son." Endure hardship as discipline; God is treating you as his children. For what children are not disciplined by their father? If you are not disciplined—and everyone undergoes discipline—then you are not legitimate, not true sons and daughters at all. Moreover, we have all had human fathers who disciplined us and we respected them for it. How much more should we submit to the Father of spirits and live!*

Just as a parent loves a child so much that he or she will discipline that child in order to teach that child, so God loves us so much that he will also discipline us. God does not want us to grow up selfish, rebellious, and spoiled. His love runs so deep that he will discipline us in order to teach us. We don't like that too much, do we?

You may hear someone say, "I thought God is love. If God is love, then he won't mind if I disobey him." How erroneous is that! Just as we would not say that a parent should ignore when a child acts selfishly or in a mean way, so it does not make sense to say that our parent God should ignore when we sin. God loves us too much to ignore our sin. Not only will God allow our sin to have consequences (such as trying drugs may lead to becoming addicted to them), but also God may actually punish us if we choose to sin. God's love for us demands that he teach us.

Thankfully, if we confess our sins to God, he will forgive us (1 John 1:9). This does not mean that we will always get out of the punishment, but we can be assured that, even though we sin and are punished, we are not thrown out of God's family. Being part of God's family means that we may rest in his love, knowing that we can depend on his faithfulness to us. It also means that we need to accept his discipline if we choose to sin. God does not allow us to stay spoiled children. God loves us too much for that.

Handing It Down

SECTION 3

DOCTRINE OF JESUS

Overview

How would you describe yourself? You may focus on the physical: the color of your hair, the shape of your body, or the size of your feet. You may describe your personality: you are friendly, introverted, sad, or intellectual. We all can describe ourselves in a variety of ways.

How would you describe Jesus? You may say he was kind, sacrificial, just, and monetarily poor. Jesus described himself as being the vine (John 15:1) and the good shepherd (John 10:11). Our theme verse for the Doctrine of Jesus helps us remember three other, very important, descriptions that Jesus used for himself. Because these three descriptions separate Jesus from all other religious leaders, we should understand them so that we can defend our faith.

I am the way: Jesus claimed to be the way, but what is he the way to? The end of the verse clarifies that question, "No one comes to the Father except through me." Jesus is the way to the Father. If anyone wants to know God and to have a relationship with God, then that person must believe in Jesus and come through him to understand God. There are not multiple ways to God, as some people teach. No, Jesus clearly stated that he is the one and only way to understand God and to have a personal relationship with God.

And the truth: As you read the gospels (Matthew, Mark, Luke, and John), you might be struck by the number of times that Jesus stated, "I tell you the truth." Jesus only speaks truth, and so as we study his words and life we will learn truth about God, truth about ourselves, truth about our world, and truth about things beyond our world. When we hear information that contradicts what Jesus taught, then that information must be wrong because Jesus is truth.

And the life: Through Jesus a person gains spiritual life which leads to eternal life. In fact, Jesus is called the author of life (Acts 3:15).

The Doctrine of Jesus will help your family understand more about this amazing God-Man, Jesus.

Theme Verse for Memorization: John 14:6

> I am the way and the truth and the life. No one comes to the Father except through me.

Let's learn who Jesus is.

Teaching 1: Jesus Is Fully God

Review Theme Verse

> I am the way and the truth and the life. No one comes to the Father except through me. (John 14:6)

DIGGING DOWN

Every culture and time period has words and phrases that are unique to that culture. Thus, if you are from a different time or culture, then it would be difficult to understand those words or phrases. For instance, here in the United States people say that they are "green with envy." Does this literally mean that the person's skin turned green because they were envious? No. People from this culture understand that it means that a person is extremely envious. Or, what about the phrase, "It is raining cats and dogs"? Do we really mean that small furry animals are falling from the sky? Not at all. When we say, "It is raining cats and dogs" we mean that it is raining very hard. Although this saying may not be understandable to those outside of the United States' culture, those who use the phrase know exactly what they mean! Every culture, including Jesus' culture, has its own unique descriptions that others might not understand.

As we found out when we learned that God is eternal, God gave himself the name, "I Am."[1] This name shows that God never began and will never end. He is eternal. Although the words, "I am" might mean something different in other cultures or time, in Jesus' culture, when those two words were put together, they were clearly a name for God. Jesus knew what this name meant, and he was not afraid to use it.

Look Up and Read John 8:56-59

> "Your father Abraham rejoiced at the thought of seeing my day; he saw it and was glad." "You are not yet fifty years old," they said to him, "and you have seen Abraham!" "Very truly I tell you," Jesus answered, "before Abraham was born, I am!" At this, they picked up stones to stone him, but Jesus hid himself, slipping away from the temple grounds.

The Jews, trying to figure out why Jesus was able to perform miracles and teach so well, challenged Jesus' authority. Then, when Jesus stated that he knew Abraham, the Jews were confused. How could Jesus, who was only in his thirties, know a man who lived 2,000 years earlier? To answer their question, Jesus called himself by a name that they clearly understood. What was the name (v. 58)? He said, "Before

Abraham was born, I am!" Knowing that the Jews understood this name, "I am" to be God's name, Jesus used it for himself. Jesus was claiming to be the eternal God. It is evident the Jews knew that Jesus was claiming to be God because they immediately tried to kill him.

By stating that he was the eternal God, Jesus claimed that he had all of the attributes, the authority, and the nature of God. Although people today may not understand that the title "I Am" is a name for God, in Jesus' day they recognized that Jesus was claiming to be God.

Some people believe Jesus was just a good man and a great teacher. But that is not what Jesus claimed. Jesus himself claimed to be the eternal God, and because of that we believe that Jesus is fully God.

> I am trying here to prevent anyone saying the really foolish thing that people often say about Him: "I'm ready to accept Jesus as a great moral teacher, but I don't accept His claim to be God." That is the one thing we must not say. A man who was merely a man and said the sort of things Jesus said would not be a great moral teacher. He would either be a lunatic-on a level with the man who says he is a poached egg-or else he would be the Devil of Hell. You must make your choice. Either this man was, and is, the Son of God: or else a madman or something worse. You can shut Him up for a fool, you can spit at Him and kill Him as a demon; or you can fall at His feet and call Him Lord and God. But let us not come with any patronizing nonsense about His being a great human teacher. He has not left that open to us. He did not intend to.
> - C.S. Lewis [2]

Questions

1. What name did Jesus use for himself?

2. Why were the Jews upset that Jesus used that name?

3. Because Jesus is God, words that we use to describe God also describe Jesus. What are some descriptions of God (powerful, wise...)?

4. Was Jesus just a good, nice man?

Digging Deeper

There is a growing belief in the world that states that Jesus, born a human baby boy, slowly became a god. As this human male made good moral choices, helped people, and lived unselfishly, he changed until he ultimately became a god. Notice that these people do not believe that Jesus is *the* God; they say Jesus is *a* god. They also believe that, depending on our choices, every one of us can become gods.

Although this belief is enticing (who of us doesn't want to become a god?), it is false. Nowhere does Scripture say that we can ever be good enough to become a god, and nowhere does it state that Jesus changed into a god as he lived his human life. In fact, it states something radically different: Jesus has and always will be THE God; it was his humanity that was added to his divinity approximately 2,000 years ago! John 1:1-3 clearly states that Jesus (the "Word") is God and that Jesus was at creation.

Look Up and Read John 1:1-3

In the beginning was the Word, and the Word was with God, and the Word was God. He was with God in the beginning. Through him all things were made; without him nothing was made that has been made.

Reread those verses substituting "Jesus" for "the Word" and you will notice how clearly Scripture states that Jesus has always been God.[3]

Look Up and Read Colossians 1:16-18

For in him [Jesus] all things were created: things in heaven and on earth, visible and invisible, whether thrones or powers or rulers or authorities; all things have been created through him and for him. He is before all things, and in him all things hold together. And he is the head of the body, the church; he is the beginning and the firstborn from among the dead, so that in everything he might have the supremacy.

Again, Scripture states that Jesus was not only at creation, but he was the principal creator. This part of the Trinity, Jesus the Son, actually was the creator of the world. If that is so, then obviously he existed long before he took on a human body as Mary's son!

Jesus himself stated, in Revelation 22:13, "I am the Alpha and the Omega, the First and the Last, the Beginning and the End." By using the first and last letters of the Greek alphabet (Alpha and Omega), and the other descriptive words of "First and Last, the Beginning and the End," Jesus claimed that he has always existed and will always exist. Jesus did not become a god while here on earth. Jesus has always been and will always be THE God.

Teaching 2: Jesus Is Fully Human

Review Theme Verse

I am the way and the truth and the life. No one comes to the Father except through me. (John 14:6)

DIGGING DOWN

* * *

Five year old Kyle was very excited. Today he was going to the hospital to see his mom and his new baby brother, Jake. Dad told him to put some things in a bag so that he would have something to do at the hospital. "Hmmm," Kyle thought, "What should I bring?" First he grabbed his baseball mitt. Perhaps Jake would like to play catch. "Does the hospital have a yard?" wondered Kyle. Next he packed his crayons and two coloring books. "That way," thought Kyle, "Jake can color in his own book and not mess up my picture." Just in case they got hungry, Kyle grabbed two apples from the kitchen, one for him and one for Jake, and put them in the bag. "Now," he thought, "I am all ready to go and meet my new baby brother."

Later, as they entered the hospital room, Kyle wondered where Jake was. Perhaps he was hiding under the bed or possibly using the bathroom. "Come close and see your baby brother," encouraged his mom. He couldn't see anything with his mom except a bundled blanket. Suddenly a very loud cry came from the blanket! What was that?

As Kyle approached, he saw a very tiny face peeping out from the blanket. This face looked human, but it was so small! His mom then showed him Jake's tiny ears, fingers, and even toes. Kyle didn't think these tiny hands would be able to hold the crayons he had brought nor would they be able to throw a ball.

Jake never said a word, but he just kept crying. His mom said, "Jake is crying because he is hungry." "Oh," thought Kyle, "I can help him with that." And he reached in his bag and pulled out an apple, handing it to his mom.

His mom shook her head, "Kyle, honey, Jake is just a baby. Babies cannot eat what big boys eat."

Again, Kyle was disappointed. Was his brother human?

* * *

Look Up and Read Luke 2:4-7

So Joseph also went up from the town of Nazareth in Galilee to Judea, to Bethlehem the town of David, because he belonged to the house and line of David. He went there to register with Mary, who was pledged to be married to him and was expecting a child. While they were there, the time came for the baby to be born, and she gave birth to her firstborn, a son. She wrapped him in cloths and placed him in a manger, because there was no guest room available for them.

Just as Kyle's baby brother was born as a tiny human, so was Jesus. Each of them had tiny fingers (too tiny to play ball with!), tiny toes, and tiny ears. Neither baby Jake nor baby Jesus could eat the food that bigger boys eat, like an apple. Baby Jesus was completely human just as any human baby is, except that Jesus never sinned. Like other human babies, Jesus didn't stay a baby, but he grew. Luke 2:40 says, "And the child [Jesus] grew and became strong." Jesus grew into a man just as other human boys do.

There are some people who believe that because Jesus was God, he could not be human. They believe he only *acted* human while he was here on earth. However, if he only acted human, then how could he have been born? How did he grow? Although it is hard to understand, we know that Jesus was completely human, and he was completely God.

Questions

1. Was Kyle's baby brother human? How do you know?
2. Was Jesus human? How can we tell?
3. Why do we believe that Jesus was completely human?
4. What would you say to someone who said that Jesus was God but not human?

Digging Deeper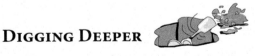

How would you define "human"? In other words, what makes a human a human? This is a very difficult question. A human does have certain physical characteristics: two hands, two eyes, a bellybutton. However, this is not what makes someone a human because, if someone were to lose one of her hands, she would still be human. The ability to think and to have emotion are also characteristics of being human, but again, if someone is mentally handicapped, that person is still a human. What is a human?

Whatever it is, we know that Jesus had it! Jesus had the physical aspects of humanity: he had feet (he walked to many places!), he hungered (Matt. 21:18), he thirsted (John 19:28). Jesus also had the emotional aspects of being a human. We know that he got angry (John 2:15), and he wept (John 11:35). Jesus was just as human as any of his contemporaries, and he was just as human as we are. If Jesus were not human, then why did Satan choose the temptations that he did? Read the account of the temptation of Jesus in Matthew.

Look Up and Read Matthew 4:1-11

> *Then Jesus was led by the Spirit into the wilderness to be tempted by the devil. After fasting forty days and forty nights, he was hungry. The tempter came to him and said, "If you are the Son of God, tell these stones to become bread." Jesus answered, "It is written: 'Man shall not live on bread alone, but on every word that comes from the mouth of God.'"*
>
> *Then the devil took him to the holy city and had him stand on the highest point of the temple. "If you are the Son of God," he said, "throw yourself down. For it is written: "'He will command his angels concerning you, and they will lift you up in their hands, so that you will not strike your foot against a stone.'" Jesus answered him, "It is also written: 'Do not put the Lord your God to the test.'"*
>
> *Again, the devil took him to a very high mountain and showed him all the kingdoms of the world and their splendor. "All this I will give you," he said, "if you will bow down and worship me." Jesus said to him, "Away from me, Satan! For it is written: 'Worship the Lord your God, and serve him only.'" Then the devil left him, and angels came and attended him.*

What were the three temptations? The first, turning a stone into bread, was only a temptation if Jesus had a human body that felt hunger. Satan understood that Jesus, as a human, would be hungry after fasting for forty days. Therefore he tempted Jesus to satisfy this human craving. In order for this to be a temptation, Jesus had to be human.

The second temptation, jumping off of the temple wall, was also based on Jesus' frail human body. If Jesus was not human, then his fall would not hurt his body, and there would be no need for angels to catch him. Again, even Satan acknowledged Jesus' humanity as he tempted him.

Although the first two temptations show the physical nature of Jesus' humanity, the third temptation shows Jesus' human emotion. "Bow down and worship me," stated Satan, "And I will give you all the kingdoms of the world." Is there a human in all of history who did not crave more fame or power? By Satan using fame and power as a temptation, we see the full emotional humanity of Jesus.

None of the three temptations would have been true temptations if Jesus had just been God who would not hunger, feel pain, or desire more power. Jesus must have been fully human (and Satan must have known that he was fully human), in order for these temptations to be effective.

Teaching 3: Jesus Is the Payment

Review Theme Verse

I am the way and the truth and the life. No one comes to the Father except through me. (John 14:6)

Doctrine of Jesus

Digging Down

Do you know what a ransom is? It is the payment that someone gives to get back something that was taken. For instance, if you owned a dog and then someone took that dog and demanded that you give him money in order to get your dog back, then you would be paying a ransom. You would be paying money in order to get back what actually belongs to you. Did you know that God paid a ransom?

God created everything including the first two people, Adam and Eve. Because God created them, they belonged to God. However, when Adam and Eve sinned by disobeying God, they became slaves to sin. They were now controlled by sin. It wasn't just Adam and Eve that became controlled by sin. Because the first people sinned, the entire human race became slaves to sin. That means you and I are slaves to sin. Although people were created by God, they were taken by sin. As a result, God decided to pay a ransom to get them back. God didn't pay money to get back what was actually his. God paid the ransom with something even more valuable.

Look Up and Read Mark 10:45

For even the Son of Man did not come to be served, but to serve, and to give his life as a ransom for many.

According to this verse, what was the ransom? God paid with Jesus' life. Even though Jesus was the Son of God, he did not come into this world so that those around him would become his slaves. About 2,000 years ago Jesus came into this world to die as a ransom for people – as a ransom for you and me. Because Jesus, the perfect, sinless God-man, died as a ransom, we have been bought back, and we can again belong to God. Just as your dog would be with you again after you paid the ransom, so people can be with God because Jesus paid the ransom with his life.

Why did God pay the ransom? Couldn't he have just forcefully taken us back? Although God is powerful enough to force us back, God is also loving. Therefore, he does not force us to be with him because he wants us to *want* to be with him. So, he sent Jesus to die in order to pay the ransom, but he waits for us to want to return to him. In other words, we now have the freedom to choose because the ransom has been paid. Jesus willingly and freely gave his life as a ransom to free us from sin and to allow us to return to God.

Questions

1. What is a ransom?
2. God paid a ransom. Why? What were people slaves to?
3. What was the ransom that God paid?
4. Do people now automatically belong back to God?

Digging Deeper

After the Israelites left their slavery in Egypt, God gave them many commands about how they were to live. Included in these commands were directions on who should be priests and what the priests should do. In Leviticus 9:7-8,15 we read of the first sin offering. This sacrifice of a calf and goat, given by the priest Aaron, was to pay for the sins of both himself and the people. God's command that the priest must offer a sacrifice to pay for the sins that the priest and the whole community had committed continued until Jesus died. Interestingly, when Jesus died, the system was not thrown out, but just revamped.

Look Up and Read Hebrews 7:23-27

Now there have been many of those priests, since death prevented them from continuing in office; but because Jesus lives forever, he has a permanent priesthood. Therefore he is able to save completely those who come to God through him, because he always lives to intercede for them. Such a high priest truly meets our need—one who is holy, blameless, pure, set apart from sinners, exalted above the heavens. Unlike the other high priests, he does not need to offer sacrifices day after day, first for his own sins, and then for the sins of the people. He sacrificed for their sins once for all when he offered himself.

The basic laws of the world, those pertaining to sin and the need for punishment or payment for sin, remain consistent through time. In Aaron's day, it was a human priest who sacrificed an animal first for himself and then for the sins of the people. When Jesus died, however, there was no longer a need for a priest on this earth to sacrifice an animal because Jesus took over the office of high priest. Since Jesus will live forever, he will be the high priest forever.

Not only is Jesus a wonderful high priest because he never has to be replaced or train someone else to do the job, but he is also the best high priest because he was sinless. Read Hebrews 7:26 again: "Such a high priest truly meets our need—one who is holy, blameless, pure, set apart from sinners, exalted above the heavens."

We are assured that this high priest is worthy to represent us and to sacrifice for us because he has never done anything wrong. In fact, he does not need to make a sacrifice for his own sins, as the former high priests needed to do. Jesus' perfection makes him the ultimate high priest.

Hebrews 7:27 gives us another reason why Jesus is the best high priest. Not only is he sinless, he also paid with something much more valuable than a calf or a goat. He sacrificed himself. His human, perfect blood paid for the sin for everyone for all time, and so the sacrifice never needs to be repeated.

There is a false teaching in the world that states that two thousand years ago there was a human named Jesus who, at his baptism, was indwelled with the divine Christ. This is the explanation for how Jesus was able to do so many miracles. Then, right before Jesus' death, the divine Christ left the human Jesus. If this is true, then what is it about Jesus' death that pays for sin? Nothing! One human dying for another does not pay for anyone's sins!

A later verse in Hebrews states, "How much more then, will the blood of Christ, who through the eternal Spirit offered himself unblemished to God, cleanse our consciences from acts that lead to death, so that we may serve the living God" (Heb. 9:14). Jesus was unblemished; he never sinned. If Jesus were truly just a man who, for a short time, was indwelled with the divine, then he could never be called sinless. Because every human sins, Jesus would have sinned during the years before the divine Christ indwelt him. Therefore, his blood would not have been unblemished; it would not be worthy to pay the ransom needed for our sins.

Our response to this wonderful news of a perfect high priest who sacrificed himself for our sins should be, as we just read in Hebrews 9:14, to want to serve the living God. Our high priest Jesus willingly paid for our sins. Let's willingly serve him.

Teaching 4: Jesus' Death for Us and for God

Review Theme Verse

I am the way and the truth and the life. No one comes to the Father except through me. (John 14:6)

Digging Down

Parent: If there is time, have each child think about what job they would like to have when they grow up. Have them act out the job while everyone else guesses what the job is. If there is not time for this pretend game, then just ask, "When you grow up, what type of job would you like to have?"

When you have a job, then you have a specific goal. If your job is being a car mechanic, then your goal might be to fix cars. If your job is being a teacher, your goal might be to help others learn. If your job is being a doctor, then your goal might be to help people be healthy. You thought of a job that you would like to have when you grow up. What is the goal of that job?

Did you know that Jesus had a job with a goal? Jesus' job was to do the work that God the Father wanted him to do. What were some of the things that Jesus did? Part of his work was to heal people, teach about God, and die on the cross. These jobs were done to reach his goals of helping people and making God famous.

Look Up and Read John 17:4

I have brought you glory on earth by finishing the work you gave me to do.

In the Bible, the word "glorify" usually means to make famous. So, Jesus wanted to make God famous on this earth by helping people. Read the verse again, but use the word "fame" instead of "glory."

As he healed people, taught people, and died on the cross, Jesus gave people more reasons to admire God. He made God famous.

Isn't that interesting? Jesus lived with the goal of making God famous. If Jesus had that goal, shouldn't we also have it? What are some ways that we could make God famous?

We could decide not to cheat on a test because God says that we shouldn't. We could tell the truth and be nice to everyone, even when they are not nice to us. Then, when someone asks us why we do these things, we could tell them that God wants us not to lie and to be nice. That is making God famous.

Two thousand years ago Jesus did the work that God wanted him to do. Some of the things he did were to heal people, to teach people, and to die on the cross. All of his work was done with the goal of making God famous.

Questions

1. What was some of the work that Jesus did?

2. What was Jesus' goal (Why did Jesus do this work?)?

3. What is another word for "glorify"?

4. What is a way that we can glorify God (that we can make God famous) like Jesus did?

Digging Deeper

If someone asked you, "Why did Jesus die on the cross?" What would you answer? Most Christians would say that Jesus died in order to save people from their sins so they could go to heaven. It is true that Jesus died to save people so that they could have eternal life (1 Cor. 15:3-4), but that is only part of the reason why he died.

During the week before his death, Jesus taught at the temple in Jerusalem. While teaching, he admitted that he did not want to undergo the humiliating, painful torture of death by crucifixion. However, he also told everyone that, even though it would be tough, he would do it. His reason for submitting himself to this death, though, was different than you may expect.

Look Up and Read John 12:27-28

> "Now my soul is troubled, and what shall I say? 'Father, save me from this hour'? No, it was for this very reason I came to this hour. Father, glorify your name!" Then a voice came from heaven, "I have glorified it, and will glorify it again."

What was the reason that Jesus gave for the death he was about to experience? "Father, glorify your name!" Previously we learned that "glory" means "fame" and so "glorify" means "to make famous." Therefore, Jesus was stating that the reason he was willing to die was so that the Father would be famous. Certainly from other passages we learn that Jesus died to save us from our sins, but this passage is very clear that Jesus also died in order for God to be famous.

Is God more famous now than before Jesus died and rose again? Think about what the world was like before Jesus' death. In Jesus' day, there were Jews, scattered throughout the Middle East, who believed in God, but beyond the Middle East few worshipped the true God. However, after Jesus died, Christianity infiltrated Europe and eventually spread to most areas of the world. God is definitely more famous now throughout the world than he was before Jesus died. In fact, in the world today the ratio of people who believe in Jesus to those who do not is almost 1:7.[4] If Jesus had not died and rose again, then Christianity would not have begun, and the worship of God may have remained confined primarily to the Jewish world. Jesus' death and resurrection did make God more famous and more admired among all the peoples of the world.

Although we are not Jesus, our lives and deaths can also make God famous. We should all ask ourselves this, "If someone knows that I am a Christian, what would they think of the God that I claim to love and serve?" Does your life display a favorable view of God, or would people look at your life and dislike, mock, or be angry at God?

Jesus lived and died both to help people and to make God famous. As followers of Jesus, we also should live and be willing to die for the fame of God.

Family Fun

Find out who your child thinks is famous. Then, spend some time together finding out more about that person. You can read a book, watch a movie, or even go to an historical site about this person. (This doesn't have to be someone that *you* think is famous. This is a great opportunity to find out who your children think is important.)

Talk about what made that person famous. Does he or she sing well, act well, or did this person do something in history? What makes someone famous? Point out that, without the marketing industry or history books, we would never have heard of that person. In fact, every time that we buy a poster with that person's picture, watch a movie, or talk about that person, we are making that person more famous! With that in mind, shouldn't we want to make God famous? Should we buy a poster about our faith, watch godly movies, and talk freely about God? Perhaps if we gave God the adoration that we give to certain people, then God would become more famous in our world.

Doctrine of Jesus

Teaching 5: Jesus' Resurrection

Review Theme Verse

I am the way and the truth and the life. No one comes to the Father except through me. (John 14:6)

Digging Down

"I saw the biggest spider in my life," exclaimed Ella, "It was bigger than my fist!" Her brother Tyler obviously didn't believe her, "Yeah, and did you see that huge snake in the backyard? It was as long as a train," he teased. Then Dad walked into the room. "Tyler, that's not a very nice thing to say," said Dad, "I was with Ella when she saw the spider, and it was bigger than any spider I have ever seen."

Do you think Tyler now believes that Ella saw a huge spider? Why?

Sometimes people say that they saw something amazing, but we do not believe them because it seems too outrageous to be real. However, if someone else says that they saw the same thing, then we probably would believe it. Because Ella's dad said that he, too, saw the spider, probably Tyler would believe it. Two people are easier to believe than one! Imagine how easy it would be to believe if five hundred people said they saw the huge spider! The Bible does not tell us about a giant spider, but it does tell us about an unbelievable event.

Look Up and Read 1 Corinthians 15:3-7

For what I received I passed on to you as of first importance: that Christ died for our sins according to the Scriptures, that he was buried, that he was raised on the third day according to the Scriptures, and that he appeared to Cephas, and then to the Twelve. After that, he appeared to more than five hundred of the brothers and sisters at the same time, most of whom are still living, though some have fallen asleep. Then he appeared to James, then to all the apostles.

In these verses, Paul wrote about some events that he thought were very important. The first was that Jesus Christ died for our sins. The second was that Jesus was buried. Paul was assuring everyone that Jesus was really dead. You would not bury someone who was still alive! Third, Jesus was raised from the dead. Jesus did not stay dead! Just think of how unbelievable this was. Who has heard of someone not staying dead!

Because this was so unbelievable, Paul knew he needed to prove that he was not the only one who had seen Jesus after he rose from the dead. So he started listing those who saw him: Cephas, the twelve, James, and five hundred others. It's as if Paul was saying, "Look, I know it is hard to believe that Jesus rose from the dead. But, if you don't believe me, ask these five hundred people! They saw him too!"

In our story, Tyler believed the spider was big because both Ella and Dad saw it. Similarly, we can know that Jesus did rise from the dead because there was not just one person who saw him. There were over five hundred people who saw him and talked with him!

When Paul wrote this down, he knew that anyone who read it could ask one of those five hundred people if they really had seen Jesus. Paul was making sure that those who doubted that Jesus rose from the dead would now believe it. This amazing miracle, that Jesus did not stay dead, is true. We can believe it because so many people saw him walking and talking after he had died and was buried. Jesus did rise from the dead!

Questions

1. Why do you believe something is true?

2. In 1 Corinthians 15:3-7 (the verses we read), what proof did Paul use to convince people that Jesus did rise from the dead?

3. Do you believe that Jesus did not stay dead? Why?

Digging Deeper

According to two early church historians, Hippolytus and Eusebius (who wrote in the third and fourth centuries, respectively) most of Jesus' disciples were killed because of their Christian faith.[5] Why were the disciples willing to die instead of renouncing their faith? People die for their Christian faith because they believe that Jesus is the Son of God, and they believe that they are saved from their sins because of Jesus' death and resurrection.

So often, when we think of how we are saved, we focus primarily on Jesus' death. Paul, in 1 Corinthians 15:3, says that "[Jesus] Christ died for our sins." It is true that Jesus' death was very important, and his death is part of what saves us from our sins. However, if Jesus had just died and stayed dead, would we still be saved?

Look Up and Read 1 Corinthians 15:17-21

And if Christ has not been raised, your faith is futile; you are still in your sins. Then those also who have fallen asleep in Christ are lost. If only for this life we have hope in Christ, we are of all people most to be pitied. But Christ has indeed been raised from the dead, the firstfruits of those who have fallen asleep. For since death came through a man, the resurrection of the dead comes also through a man.

According to these verses, we would not be saved from the penalty of our sins if Jesus had not risen from the dead. This is one reason why we celebrate not only the death but also the resurrection of Jesus.

Without the resurrection, Jesus' death was just a man dying; there was no miracle surrounding it. Jesus needed to beat death in order to take away the penalty of our sins and to allow us to live forever with him.

Verse 20 says that "Jesus is the firstfruits of those who have fallen asleep." The first fruit is the fruit that comes first in a harvest. It is not the only fruit, it is just the first. Jesus was the first one to be raised so that he will never die. But he was not the only one who will live forever! Because Jesus conquered death he was the first one to live forever, and we are the rest of the harvest! This is one reason why the resurrection is so important. Because Jesus is alive, he made it possible for everyone who believes in him to also live forever with him.

Paul stated, "If Christ has not been raised, your faith is futile; you are still in your sins" (1 Cor. 15:17). Because the apostles were sure of Jesus' resurrection, they knew that their faith was not futile or useless. Thus, they were willing to die for their faith. Knowing that they would live forever with Jesus, these men received hope and courage from Jesus' resurrection.

We have that same hope of a future life because of Jesus' resurrection. Jesus' death and resurrection saves us from the penalty of our sins and gives us hope so that we do not need to be afraid of death.

Teaching 6: Jesus Is Still Living

Review Theme Verse

> *I am the way and the truth and the life. No one comes to the Father except through me. (John 14:6)*

Digging Down

Have you looked at a cloud and noticed that it has the shape of an animal, a ship, or something else? What shapes have you seen in the clouds? Looking at the clouds and trying to see different shapes is a fun game to play! (If you have time right now, you could go outside and look at the shapes of the clouds and see what you can imagine!) When we look at the sky, there are certain things that we expect to see there, like clouds, birds, and airplanes. Although we may think a cloud has the shape of a boat, we don't actually expect to see a boat floating through the air. We may have seen clouds that looked like an elephant, but we would never actually expect to see an elephant walking around in the air!

Did you know that 2,000 years ago there was a group of men who saw a real man go up into the clouds? This man who went up into the clouds was not in an airplane nor was he wearing some sort of rocket-shoes. This man, standing with a group of his friends on a mountain, just rose into the air and disappeared into the clouds! Who was this man? Jesus.

Look Up and Read Acts 1:9-11

After he [Jesus] said this, he was taken up before their very eyes, and a cloud hid him from their sight. They were looking intently up into the sky as he was going, when suddenly two men dressed in white stood beside them. "Men of Galilee," they said, "why do you stand here looking into the sky? This same Jesus, who has been taken from you into heaven, will come back in the same way you have seen him go into heaven."

When Jesus was about thirty-three years old people killed him by crucifying him. Three days later Jesus came back to life. He was not dead anymore! Then, for forty days Jesus walked around, teaching his friends more about God. He wanted them to know what it meant to be part of God's family and about the kingdom of God. At the end of those forty days, Jesus walked up on a mountain with his friends. While standing with them, he suddenly was "taken up" into the sky where he disappeared in a cloud. We call this Jesus' ascension. Jesus ascended, which means he rose, into the sky. Wouldn't that be surprising?

As Jesus disappeared, his friends kept looking at the sky. Suddenly two angels, dressed in white, appeared to the men and told them that Jesus had gone to heaven. Jesus was still alive, but now Jesus would live in heaven, not on earth. Then they gave some very exciting news. Someday Jesus will come back through the clouds.

Won't that be amazing? We know that Jesus died once, while on earth, but he did not stay dead. After coming back to life, Jesus lived for forty days on earth, and then he went to heaven where he lives today. Someday Jesus will come back through the air just as he went up.

Now when you look at the clouds in the sky and imagine all those animals or ships, you can also think about Jesus. Someday this very real God-man will come through the clouds. That's something to look forward to!

Questions

1. Is Jesus alive right now, or is he dead?

2. Where does Jesus live now?

3. What do we call Jesus' rising into the sky?

4. When we look at the clouds, of what can we be reminded?

Digging Deeper

When you think of Jesus, what do you imagine him looking like? Perhaps, in your mind, he looks like a shepherd with a sheep in his arms. Or maybe he looks like a 30-year-old Middle-Eastern itinerate preacher sitting next to God's throne. Another image could be a fatherly figure standing with open arms. Daniel, a Jew in the Old Testament, saw Jesus as a king to whom the world bows.

God gave Daniel many different visions prophesying future events. One such vision was when God, the Ancient of Days, gave all ruling authority to someone who, to Daniel, looked like a man.

Look Up and Read Daniel 7:13-14

In my vision at night I looked, and there before me was one like a son of man, coming with the clouds of heaven. He approached the Ancient of Days and was led into his presence. He was given authority, glory and sovereign power; all nations and peoples of every language worshiped him. His dominion is an everlasting dominion that will not pass away, and his kingdom is one that will never be destroyed.

All people, from every language group, served this king as he ruled his eternal kingdom. Who is this leader who looked like a "son of man?"

In Scriptures written before Daniel 7, when the term "Son of Man" was used, it meant a human person. David, in his psalms often referred to himself or other men as a "son of man." In the book of Ezekiel God repeatedly called Ezekiel a "son of man" because Ezekiel was human. So, when Daniel stated that this ruler looked like a "Son of Man" we know that this meant that this ruler did not look like some beast with wings or hundreds of eyes. No, this ruler to whom

God gave authority looked like a man. However, Daniel's use of the term completely changed the way the term was subsequently used. No longer in the Scriptures or with the Jews did it mean just a human. Now everyone understood "Son of Man" to mean the ruler of the universe, the person to whom all nations will bow.

All four gospel writers, Matthew, Mark, Luke, and John, documented Jesus referring to himself as the Son of Man. When he did so, he was referring to the Daniel 7 passage where the Son of Man was given authority to rule. When Jesus used the term "Son of Man" for himself, he was describing his power to forgive sins (Matt. 9:6), his ability to rise from the dead (Mark 8:31), his ability to grant eternal life to his followers (John 6:27), and his return as he descends on the clouds (Luke 21:27). All of these show Jesus' authority and power to rule over an eternal kingdom. All of these admit that Jesus is the eternal ruler mentioned in Daniel 7.

Jesus lived on earth and identified himself as the Son of Man who will live forever, ruling an eternal kingdom while being worshiped by people from all language groups. Do we believe this is true? If we do, then we should not think of Jesus as just a kindly shepherd who opens his arms to accept his wayward sheep. Jesus is our loving shepherd; however Jesus is also a king. We must remember that, as a king, Jesus demands and deserves our worship, adoration, and respect.

Teaching 7: Preparation for Jesus' Return

Review Theme Verse

> *I am the way and the truth and the life. No one comes to the Father except through me. (John 14:6)*

DIGGING DOWN

Who lives in your house with you? Perhaps one or two parents, your grandparents, your brothers, your sisters, an aunt or uncle, and your pet live with you. Some people live with many people; others live with only a few. Sometimes we choose whom we live with, but there are times when we do not have a choice. Did you know that Jesus wants to live with us forever? Right now Jesus is in heaven preparing a house where everyone who is in his family can live!

Look Up and Read John 14:2-3

> *My Father's house has many rooms; if that were not so, would I have told you that I am going there to prepare a place for you? And if I go and prepare a place for you, I will come back and take you to be with me that you also may be where I am.*

We know that Jesus died, became alive again, and then ascended into heaven. In these verses, Jesus told his friends about one of the jobs he would have while he is in heaven. What is that job? Jesus said that he would prepare a place in his Father's house for all of his family to live. He promised to come back and get his whole family. Then we will all live with him forever.

These verses comfort us because we know that, if we are part of God's family, we can look forward to a wonderful life even after our life on earth is over. They also assure us that Jesus is alive and working. When Jesus died on the cross, he did not stay dead. No, Jesus rose from the dead and then, without dying again, he went up to heaven. Right now Jesus is alive in heaven preparing a place for each of us to live. When we are part of God's family, we can be sure that we serve and love not a dead man or a man-made idol, but we serve a living God. Jesus is living right now in heaven, preparing a place for you to

Handing It Down

live, and he will come back and get everyone who is part of his family so that we all can live forever with him!

Right now you might live with only a few people or with many people, but when Jesus returns and we get to heaven, we will live with all of God's family, including Jesus, forever!

Questions

1. Is Jesus alive right now, or is he dead?

2. What is one way that we can know that Jesus has not forgotten about us?

3. Who will live in the house that Jesus is preparing?

Digging Deeper

When your teacher announces a test for the next day, what is your reaction? Do you inwardly groan and know that you are going to have a long night of studying ahead of you? Or do you shrug your shoulders and figure that you don't need to prepare? There are tests that we do not need to study for, but there are other tests that we might fail if we do not study for them.

Jesus told a story of ten women who had a choice about how they were going to prepare for an upcoming event. Although they were not preparing for a test, they were preparing for something very important.

Look Up and Read Matthew 25:1-13

> *At that time the kingdom of heaven will be like ten virgins who took their lamps and went out to meet the bridegroom. Five of them were foolish and five were wise. The foolish ones took their lamps but did not take any oil with them. The wise ones, however, took oil in jars*

> *along with their lamps. The bridegroom was a long time in coming, and they all became drowsy and fell asleep.*
>
> *At midnight the cry rang out: "Here's the bridegroom! Come out to meet him!" Then all the virgins woke up and trimmed their lamps. The foolish ones said to the wise, "Give us some of your oil; our lamps are going out." "No," they replied, "there may not be enough for both us and you. Instead, go to those who sell oil and buy some for yourselves." But while they were on their way to buy the oil, the bridegroom arrived. The virgins who were ready went in with him to the wedding banquet. And the door was shut. Later the others also came. "Lord, Lord," they said, "open the door for us!" But he replied, "Truly I tell you, I don't know you." Therefore keep watch, because you do not know the day or the hour.*

These ten women prepared for a bridegroom to come. All night they waited, but it got later and later and this man didn't come. Eventually they all fell asleep. Suddenly, they woke up to shouts as people announced the bridegroom's arrival. Five women were prepared for this event; they had all the oil for their lamps that they needed. However, five were not prepared. While they slept, their oil had run out, and thus they needed to run to the market to buy more oil. Because they were gone when the banquet started, they were completely left out.

Why did Jesus tell this story? What event was he telling us to be prepared for? Jesus told this story to warn his listeners, including us, that we must be prepared for when he will come back. Right now Jesus is in heaven, but he will come back to earth someday, riding on the clouds (Luke 21:27). This is the event that we must keep watch for. This is the event that we might not be ready for if we just shrug our shoulders and decide that we don't care.

The difficult thing is, we don't know when Jesus will return. When a teacher gives a test, usually we have a warning allowing us to study for it. Jesus' return is like a teacher telling you that sometime this year you will have a very important test. If you do not pass that test, then you will not be able to go on to the next grade. Without knowing the date of the test, there is a chance that you would start out the school year studying every night for the test, just in case it is given the next day. However, as the days, weeks, and months go by, you may become more lax in your studying, perhaps skipping a day or two here or there and then skipping a whole week and then a whole month. At last the day would come when the teacher hands you the test. If you hadn't studied, how prepared would you be?

Jesus told us that he will come back. However, he did not tell us when that event will happen. He only told us to "keep watch, because you do not know the day or the hour" (Matt. 25:13). Just as we would need to be diligent and keep studying for an upcoming important test, we must be diligent and keep our lives ready for Jesus to come back. It would be awful to have Jesus come back at a time when we are shrugging our shoulders and not caring.

Are you ready for Jesus to come back? It could be any day and any hour. Through the story of these ten women, Jesus warned us to keep watch and be ready for his return. Are you prepared?

Teaching 8: Jesus Is the Crux

Review Theme Verse

I am the way and the truth and the life. No one comes to the Father except through me. (John 14:6)

Digging Down

Where is the closest gate to your house? Perhaps there is a gate that lets people into your yard or a gate that lets your pet out of its pen or carrier, or perhaps the nearest gate is far away from your house. What is the purpose of a gate? The gate is the door that allows someone or something to go into and out of an area. The gate is also for security. In other words, the gate keeps the unwanted out while letting the wanted in. Did you know that Jesus says that he is a gate?

Look Up and Read John 10:9

> *I [Jesus] am the gate; whoever enters through me will be saved. They will come in and go out, and find pasture.*

Jesus said that he is the gate that people must go through in order to be saved. What does this mean?

Because the first people, Adam and Eve, sinned, all people are born with sin (Rom. 5:17). This sin keeps us away from God, and we need a gate to help us get to God.

Imagine it like this: Everyone has sin, and so we all live in a dark, giant field. In this field there is no love, joy, or peace because God, who brings love, joy, and peace, is not in the field. Obviously, we do not want to stay in this dark field!

Off in the distance we see a fenced-in house that is filled with light. The people in that house are part of God's family, and so they are laughing and having a great time because they no longer live in the dark field of sin. We start searching, trying to get into the building.

As we search, we notice a gate. In order to get to the house, all we have to do is walk through that gate. It seems easy enough! As we approach the gate, we notice that most people are not walking through the gate. Instead, they are trying to climb over the fence, dig under the fence, or look for a way around the fence. Every time they try to climb over, they fall off the fence. Every time they try to dig under, they hit a rock and can't dig anymore. As they try to get around the fence, they just keep walking in circles because there is no other way into the house. If you want to get into the house, into God's family, you must go through the gate.

Who is the gate? Jesus. Every person who wants to be part of God's family must go through the Jesus-gate. That means we must believe that Jesus died and rose again to forgive our sins. It is easy to get into God's family, but most people refuse to believe those things about Jesus. They refuse to use the Jesus-gate.

Some people say there are many ways to have a relationship with God. But, just as our memory verse says, Jesus is the only way, the only truth, and the only life. People must believe and depend on Jesus to have their sins forgiven and to be in God's family. Each person must go through the Jesus-gate.

Questions

1. Why does everyone start in the dark field of sin?
2. In the verse we read, John 10:9, what does Jesus say he is?
3. We can be in God's family (get into the light house) if we do what?
4. Are there other ways to be in God's family besides believing in Jesus?

Digging Deeper

Movies and television are full of heroes who valiantly fight off villains while the virtuous but helpless people watch with awe. People like strong, powerful heroes, whether those heroes are invented for entertainment or are real people. When someone shows physical or financial power, people will often follow because we all want a strong hero.

What would we think of a hero who was beaten up, kicked, and spit on by his adversaries? Would people be drawn to a hero who did not pull out a laser gun or battle ax to defend his life but who allowed himself to get beat up by the villagers? Instead of being rich and famous, this hero dies so poor he is buried in a borrowed grave. Would we admire this kind of hero?

Did you know that Christianity tells the story of this hero? Jesus did not bring his wealth and power to our world. Instead, he entered as a human. He did not brandish a sword while riding a white stallion through the streets of Jerusalem. He allowed himself to die. And it wasn't even for the virtuous innocent that he died. He died for us who are sinners, who selfishly live for our own safety and good.

"But God demonstrates his own love for us in this: While we were still sinners, Christ died for us." (Rom. 5:8) Jesus is a hero not because he defended the innocent but because he died for the sinner.

Look Up and Read John 10:11

> I [Jesus] am the good shepherd. The good shepherd lays down his life for the sheep.

Our hero, our leader, our shepherd, took care of us by allowing himself to get beat up and die. Jesus was whipped, punched, spit on, mocked, humiliated, and nailed to rough lumber because he loved us even though we are selfish and evil. That kind of hero deserves our adoration.

Too often we spend our time and money adoring earthly heroes such as famous movie stars, athletes, or even kind, generous people who defend the innocent. Some of us even adore fictional characters!

How much time do we spend adoring, worshipping, and learning about Jesus, the hero who loved us so much that he died for us?

Jesus is the crux of Christianity because he is the innocent hero who willingly died to save an unadoring audience. Jesus is the ultimate hero who deserves our adoration and worship.

Teaching 9: Jesus Loves Us

Review Theme Verse

I am the way and the truth and the life. No one comes to the Father except through me. (John 14:6)

DIGGING DOWN

We all have muscles. Right now show your arm muscles! Every person has muscles, but at the same time every person is also weak. Think about what you can lift. You may be able to lift a chair but not a huge brick wall. You may be able to move your dog but not your house. Although we all have muscles, none of us are so strong that we can lift a planet. People are strong, but there is a limit to our strength.

Sometimes we feel strong with our arms, and sometimes we feel strong with our minds. We may know how to do math very well, but there is a limit to our mental strength because there are some math problems we cannot figure out. When we face that type of problem, we may feel weak.

We also may feel strong or weak with our emotions. When we are happy then we feel strong, but when someone is mean to us, then we may feel weak and sad. As Christians we may feel strong when we make choices that God would like. Then we may feel weak when we lie or disobey our parents. We know that Jesus wants us to obey him, but sometimes we feel weak because it seems hard to obey.

Jesus knows that sometimes we feel strong, and sometimes we feel weak, and he wants to help us!

Look Up and Read Matthew 11:28-30

> *Come to me [Jesus], all you who are weary and burdened, and I will give you rest. Take my yoke upon you and learn from me, for I am gentle and humble in heart, and you will find rest for your souls. For my yoke is easy and my burden is light.*

When a farmer uses oxen to pull a wagon or plow, he attaches two oxen together with a yoke. The farmer knows that both oxen, by working together, can pull heavier loads than one ox alone. The strength of two oxen is obviously stronger than the strength of one.

Jesus used this image of a yoke to show that he wants to help us when we feel weak. Since he is powerful enough to pick up a planet or help us when we are sad, we know that with his help we can get through any situation.

Jesus also knows that sometimes it is difficult to tell the truth, to obey our parents, and to live so that Jesus becomes famous and loved. Sometimes it is hard to be different than our friends. However, in these verses Jesus says that his burden is light. When you feel that it is hard to be a Christian, remember that Jesus wants to help you.

Jesus doesn't ask us to pick up planets, but he does want us to love him and obey him. However, because he loves us, Jesus will help us obey him if we ask him.

The next time you are sad or feel weak because it is so hard to obey Jesus, remember that Jesus loves you and wants to help you. Pray and ask him to help you. He will because he loves you.

Questions

1. When is a time that you felt strong?

2. When is a time that you felt weak?

3. Who will help us when we feel weak?

4. Why does Jesus help us when we feel weak?

Digging Deeper

Did you know that the Pacific Ocean is the largest ocean on earth, and it covers about 30 percent of the earth? That means you could put the United States in it fifteen times![6] The Mountain with the highest elevation on earth is Mount Everest, and it is 29,028 feet (8,848 meters) above sea level.[7] The deepest part of an ocean is the Mariana Trench in the Pacific Ocean. There the bottom of the ocean is 35,840 feet (10,911 meters) below sea level.[8] That means you could put Mount Everest in the Mariana Trench and there would still be one mile of water above it!

The earth is huge, with high peaks, low depths, and wide oceans. When we see oceans, large deserts, the huge sky, and high mountain peaks, we get an idea of how much love Jesus has for us.

Paul wrote in Ephesians 3:17b-18, "And I pray that you, being rooted and established in love, may have power, together with all the Lord's holy people, to grasp how wide and long and high and deep is the love of Christ."

How much does Jesus love us? Jesus loves us so much that, when you look at the widest ocean, you can know that Jesus loves you more than that. When you think about the deep Mariana Trench, you can know that Jesus loves you more than that. When you gaze at the tall Mount Everest, you can know that Jesus loves you more than that. Jesus' love for you is deeper, wider, higher than anything we can imagine!

That is a huge love. Do you believe that Jesus loves you that much? Sometimes we focus on the hardships we have and the lessons Jesus wants to teach us. Therefore we may begin to view Jesus as someone we must appease so our lives do not get too difficult. We may view Jesus as a teacher who has high standards, one who is constantly trying to challenge us. But there is another view of Jesus that we need to understand.

Jesus loves us, and nothing can separate us from that love.

Look Up and Read Romans 8:35-39

> *Who shall separate us from the love of Christ? Shall trouble or hardship or persecution or famine or nakedness or danger or sword? As it is written: "For your sake we face death all day long; we are considered as sheep to be slaughtered."*
>
> *No, in all these things we are more than conquerors through him who loved us. For I am convinced that neither death nor life, neither angels nor demons, neither the present nor the future, nor any powers, neither height nor depth, nor anything else in all creation, will be able to separate us from the love of God that is in Christ Jesus our Lord.*

These verses acknowledge that we will have trouble in our lives. However, in the midst of that trouble we can be sure that nothing can take away Jesus' love for us.

Because of Jesus' vast, deep, enduring love for us, we can confidently face all trials, knowing that this love is deeper, wider, and higher than we can imagine. Jesus' love will never leave us, and it will help us be "more than conquerors" as we face the trials of our lives (Rom. 8:37).

The next time you look at an ocean, the sky, or a mountain peak, remember that Jesus loves you higher, wider, and deeper than that.

SECTION  4

DOCTRINE OF THE HOLY SPIRIT

Overview

Have you ever seen a marching band perform? This diverse group of individuals seeks to act as one whole. One way they accomplish that melding is by coordinating their step to match everyone else's step. In fact, if someone is out of step with the group, or if someone chooses to branch off and go his own way, that person becomes very noticeable, and the entire dynamic of the group is disrupted. By working hard to stay in step with each other, the band creates a beautiful, unified group. When we understand the picture of the marching band, we get a glimpse into how we walk with the Holy Spirit.

Our theme verse says that we are to "keep in step with the Spirit." As the Holy Spirit leads, we need to follow. As the Holy Spirit teaches, we need to learn. We must choose to act and think how the Spirit wants us to act and think. By refusing to march to our own beat, we work to keep in step with the Spirit. If we are not in step, then we are disrupting the beautiful whole of what God would like to do in our lives, and, instead of glorifying God, we bring shame on the name of our God.

As Christians, we say that we desire to follow God. Often, however, we actually choose not to follow God. We choose to be out of step with the Holy Spirit. Our eyes and mind wander into sin. We live with anger, and our tongues hurt others with slander and gossip. There are many ways that we impair the working of the Spirit, and when we choose to sin, we are not living by the Spirit.

When we live by the Holy Spirit, we choose to live as God would want us to live, and we keep in step with the Spirit. The Holy Spirit wants to work in our lives so that we glorify God and have true joy, peace, and patience. However, if we refuse to keep in step with the Spirit, we are choosing to disrupt the work that God would like to do.

Theme Verse for Memorization: Galatians 5:25

Since we live by the Spirit, let us keep in step with the Spirit.

Let's learn how to keep in step with the Spirit.

Teaching 1: The Holy Spirit Is Fully God

Review Theme Verse

Since we live by the Spirit, let us keep in step with the Spirit. (Galatians 5:25)

DIGGING DOWN

Sometimes we use two words to mean the same thing. For instance, if you want a cookie, you could say, "Mom, did you make Snickerdoodles? May I have one of the cookies?" Here you used two words, "snickerdoodle" and "cookie" to mean the same thing. Because we know that a snickerdoodle is a cookie, we understand that we can use the word cookie to describe a snickerdoodle. Can you think of other examples, using two different words to mean the same thing (e.g. "collie" and "dog")?

The Bible tells an interesting story about a man, Ananias, and his wife, Sapphira, who decided to lie to God. This couple sold some property, kept some of the money from the sale, and then gave the rest of the money to the church. There was no problem with them keeping some of the money, except that they told Peter they were giving *all* of the money. When Peter asked them if they were giving all of the money, they chose to lie.

Peter told them that they were not lying to people, but to the Holy Spirit. Interestingly, when he was talking to Ananias, Peter used two different names for the Holy Spirit. See if you can pick out what two names he used.

Look Up and Read Acts 5:1-5

> *Now a man named Ananias, together with his wife Sapphira, also sold a piece of property. With his wife's full knowledge he kept back part of the money for himself, but brought the rest and put it at the apostles' feet. Then Peter said, "Ananias, how is it that Satan has so filled your heart that you have lied to the Holy Spirit and have kept for yourself some of the money you received for the land? Didn't it belong to you before it was sold? And after it was sold, wasn't the money at your disposal? What made you think of doing such a thing? You have not lied just to human beings but to God." When Ananias heard this, he fell down and died. And great fear seized all who heard what had happened.*

What were the names that Peter used for the Holy Spirit? "Holy Spirit" (v. 3) and "God" (v. 4) were the two names that Peter used. Peter used the name "God" for the Holy Spirit, so we understand that the Holy Spirit is not just a force, a power, or even an angel, but the Holy Spirit is actually God. Because the Holy Spirit is God, the Holy Spirit can do everything we say God the Father and Jesus the Son can do. The Holy Spirit is just as powerful as the Father and Jesus are, and the Holy Spirit loves people just as they do. Everything that God is, the Holy Spirit is, because the Holy Spirit is God.

Just as we understand that a snickerdoodle is a cookie, and we can use either one of those names for the snack we want to eat, so we can use the words "Holy Spirit" and "God" to mean the Holy Spirit. Why? Because the Holy Spirit is God. However, just as the snickerdoodle is not the only type of cookie, so the Holy Spirit is not the only person of God.

God is three persons, the Trinity: God the Father, Jesus the Son, and the Holy Spirit. All three of them are fully, completely God. Because they make up the one God, we say that we worship one God with three persons: God the Father, Jesus the Son, and the Holy Spirit. Some people do not believe that the Holy Spirit is God, but we know that he is God because Peter used both names, "God" and "Holy Spirit," when he talked about the Holy Spirit.

Questions

1. What are two names that Peter used for the Holy Spirit?
2. Say some words that describe God.
3. Do those words describe the Holy Spirit? Why?
4. Who are the three Persons in the Trinity?

Digging Deeper

We say that the Holy Spirit is fully God. But what does that mean? It means that the Holy Spirit is as much God as God the Father and Jesus the Son are God.

For instance, God the Father and Jesus the Son are eternal. They have always existed and always will exist. The Bible tells us that the Holy

Spirit is also eternal (Heb. 9:14). In fact, in Genesis 1:2, his existence is mentioned in the description of the world before creation, "Now the earth was formless and empty, darkness was over the surface of the deep, and the Spirit of God was hovering over the waters." The Holy Spirit is eternal.

Another description of God is that he is omnipresent, meaning God is everywhere. David, in Psalm 139:7, reflects on the Holy Spirit's omnipresence as he asks the rhetorical question, "Where can I go from your Spirit? Where can I flee from your presence?" In the next few verses he admits that, no matter where he attempts to go, the Spirit will be there (Ps. 139:7-10). Because the Spirit is omnipresent, there is nowhere we can hide!

The Holy Spirit is also powerful. He creates life (Ps. 104:30, Job 33:4). He also can give humans strength (Judg. 14:6), hope (Rom. 15:13), and the ability to love (2 Tim. 1:7). The Holy Spirit is powerful enough to help people just as God the Father and Jesus the Son can help people.

From these verses we know that the Holy Spirit is not an angel, an abstract force, or a powerful wind. The Holy Spirit is God who is eternal, has all knowledge (omniscient), exists everywhere (omnipresent), and is powerful (omnipotent). The Holy Spirit is God just as God the Father and Jesus the Son are God.

All three persons of the Trinity: God the Father, God the Son, and God the Holy Spirit, appear at Jesus' baptism. Jesus was in the water, God the Holy Spirit appeared in the form of a dove, and the spectators heard God the Father's voice (Matt. 3:16-17). We serve one God who consists of three distinct persons: God the Father, God the Son, and God the Holy Spirit. Therefore, the Holy Spirit is completely God.

Handing It Down

Family Fun

Using the letters in the words, "God the Father, Jesus the Son, and the Holy Spirit," make as many words describing God as possible. For instance, you could make the words, "just," "trust" (we can trust him), and even "sinless." After you make as many words as you can, add to your list by brainstorming more descriptions of God!

Teaching 2: The Holy Spirit's Personhood

Review Theme Verse

Since we live by the Spirit, let us keep in step with the Spirit. (Galatians 5:25)

Digging Down

Often it is easier to say something mean about someone than to say something nice. Right now have everyone say something nice or something they like about each person with you. Remember, don't say something mean or hurtful. Make sure that what you say is nice.

Sometimes it is difficult to say nice things. At times our mouth is very hard to control because it wants to say something mean or hurtful to someone or about someone. We may even spread rumors and tell lies about someone else. When our friends are being mean to someone, it can be very easy for us to join in and be mean too. There are other times when we get so angry at someone that we say or do something hurtful.

When we hurt someone by saying or doing something mean, we are sinning. Did you know that when we sin we grieve the Holy Spirit? This means that the Holy Spirit actually gets sad when we sin.

Look Up and Read Ephesians 4:29-32

> *Do not let any unwholesome talk come out of your mouths, but only what is helpful for building others up according to their needs, that it may benefit those who listen. And do not grieve the Holy Spirit of God, with whom you were sealed for the day of redemption. Get rid of all bitterness, rage and anger, brawling and slander, along with every form of malice. Be kind and compassionate to one another, forgiving each other, just as in Christ God forgave you.*

What are the sins, in these verses, that the Holy Spirit grieves about? We know that our anger and the mean words we say can hurt someone. But our sin does more than hurt people. These verses state that, when we sin, the Holy Spirit becomes sad. So, every time we are mean to someone, we make the Holy Spirit unhappy.

Because the Holy Spirit feels emotion such as sadness, just as people feel emotion, we say that the Holy Spirit is a person. This does not mean, however, that the Holy Spirit sins like people or even has a body like a person. No, the Holy Spirit is God just as Jesus is God, so the Holy Spirit does not sin. The Holy Spirit is a person because he can think, he has emotion like sadness, and he can make decisions.

The next time you say something mean or want to hurt someone, stop and think about what you are doing. Remember that you are making the Holy Spirit sad. If you do say something mean about someone, admit that you have sinned and decide that you will try to only say kind words. Then you will make the Holy Spirit happy!

Questions

1. Does the Holy Spirit become sad?
2. What makes the Holy Spirit sad?
3. Why do we say that the Holy Spirit is a person?
4. What are ways that the Holy Spirit is not like people?

Digging Deeper

The Library of Congress in the United States claims that it is the largest library in the world. This enormous library in Washington D.C. has one hundred forty-five million items in it, and so it has over seven hundred forty-five miles of shelves![1] There is quite a bit of information in that library!

People love to learn. That is one characteristic that defines us as a person. Besides having intellect, a person has emotion and a will. People can feel sadness, joy, anticipation, worry, excitement, and anger. People can also make decisions and have opinions. We can choose what to do with our time and try to convince others to act, think, and believe as we do. All of us have this individual will.

Because each member of the Trinity, God the Father, Jesus the Son, and the Holy Spirit, displays the three characteristics of intellect, emotion, and will, we say that each one is a person: the person of the Father, the person of the Son, and the person of the Spirit. Being a person in this sense does not mean that they are sinful, nor does it mean that they have the physical characteristics of humans. It means that they have the personhood characteristics of intellect, emotion, and will.

Earlier we looked up Ephesians 4:30 where we discovered that the Holy Spirit becomes sad. This is one example of the Holy Spirit's emotion.

Look Up and Read 1 Corinthians 2:11

> *For who knows a person's thoughts except their own spirit within them? In the same way no one knows the thoughts of God except the Spirit of God.*

The Holy Spirit knows the thoughts of God and thus we understand that he has the knowledge and understanding of God. The Library of Congress, with its one hundred forty-five million items, is no challenge to the intellect of the Holy Spirit!

The Holy Spirit has emotion and intellect. The Spirit has another characteristic of a person: will.

Look Up and Read 1 Corinthians 12:11

> *All these are the work of one and the same Spirit, and he distributes them to each one, just as he determines.*

This verse comes after a long passage about gifts that the Holy Spirit gives. Did you notice who determines what gifts to give to people? It is the Holy Spirit who decides who gets which gifts. The Holy Spirit has the will to choose; the Spirit is not an impersonal force or even an angel, but the Holy Spirit is an intelligent being with emotion and will. Because the Spirit has these characteristics of personhood, we say that the Holy Spirit is a person. The Spirit is the Third Person in the Trinity because God the Father, Jesus the Son, and the Holy Spirit all have the personhood characteristics of intellect, emotion, and will.

Teaching 3: The Holy Spirit Is Throughout the Bible

Review Theme Verse

Since we live by the Spirit, let us keep in step with the Spirit. (Galatians 5:25)

DIGGING DOWN

Have you ever had a problem that you did not know how to handle? Perhaps someone was mean to you, and you did not know what to do. Or, perhaps you wanted to be friends with someone, but you were not sure how to start. Maybe schoolwork was hard, or you were not sure what to do for a school project. Many times we need advice and we do not know where to get it.

Did you know that the Holy Spirit wants to help us when we have problems? There are many places in the Bible where we read how the Holy Spirit helps and teaches people. Jesus himself tells us that we have the Holy Spirit to help us.

Look Up and Read John 14:26

But the Advocate, the Holy Spirit, whom the Father will send in my name, will teach you all things and will remind you of everything I have said to you.

In this verse, Jesus told his followers that they will have the Holy Spirit to help them after Jesus goes back up to heaven. Look at the verse again, and try to list all of the things that Jesus said the Holy Spirit would do for his friends and for those who are part of God's family.

The Holy Spirit is called our Advocate. An advocate listens to and understands the person he is helping. The Holy Spirit, as our advocate, will always be with us to listen to us and to help us. He never leaves us, so we know that anytime we need help, the Holy Spirit is right there!

This verse also states that the Holy Spirit will teach us and remind us of what Jesus said. We have, living with us, the Holy Spirit who will give us advice and help us even when we are faced with tough decisions.

The Bible tells us about a man named Paul who went to many different cities and countries telling people about Jesus. When he traveled, he always asked the Holy Spirit where he should go, and he would follow what the Holy Spirit wanted him to do. In Acts 16:6-7, the Bible says there were some places where the Holy Spirit would not allow Paul to teach! Just as Paul obeyed the Holy Spirit and got advice from the Spirit, so we too can ask the Holy Spirit to help us and give us advice.

Many times in the New Testament, we read about the Holy Spirit living in people who are part of God's family. Just as Jesus' friends, Paul, and other Christians in the New Testament had the Holy Spirit with them, we too have the Holy Spirit with us all the time.

Questions

1. What did Jesus say the Holy Spirit would do?

2. Who can we get help and advice from?

3. How do we get help and advice from the Holy Spirit?

Digging Deeper

King David, an avid musician and song-writer, composed many songs praising God and lamenting his own circumstances. Psalm 51, written after he was confronted for committing adultery with Bathsheba, displays his deep sorrow for his sin.

Look Up and Read Psalm 51:10-11

Create in me a pure heart, O God, and renew a steadfast spirit within me. Do not cast me from your presence or take your Holy Spirit from me.

In his distress, David cries out for forgiveness and pleads with God, begging him not to take the Holy Spirit away. Why would David think that God would take the Holy Spirit away?

In the Old Testament, before Jesus' death and resurrection, the Holy Spirit did not indwell all of God's followers all of the time. That was not his role. Instead, the Holy Spirit helped people at specific times and for specific purposes. For instance, God filled Bezalel with the Holy Spirit so that Bezalel had amazing artistic skill which he used to construct articles for the tabernacle (Exod. 31:2-5).

Another example of the Holy Spirit entering someone at a specific time, for a specific purpose, is in Numbers 24:2-3, when Balaam prophesied about Israel. Although the Spirit of God gave Balaam the words to say in this instance, the Holy Spirit did not continually dwell within Balaam.

The Judges of Israel often relied upon the Spirit of God as they fought. Gideon received the Holy Spirit as he rallied forces for a battle against the Midianites and Amalekites (Judg. 6:33-34). Jephthah received the Holy Spirit as he went against the Ammonites (Judg. 11:29), and the Holy Spirit came upon Samson as he defended his own life against a lion's attack (Judg. 14:6).

Although we read that the Holy Spirit was very active in Old Testament times, the Spirit did not continually indwell God's followers during that time period. Jesus declared, however, that was going to change.

We read, in John 14:16, Jesus telling his followers, "And I will ask the Father, and he will give you another advocate to help you and be with you forever." Jesus promised that the Holy Spirit would now indwell believers forever. No longer does a believer need to be concerned, as David had been, that God would take away the Holy Spirit. Once a person believes in Jesus, joining God's family, that person receives the Holy Spirit, and the Holy Spirit will stay with that person forever.

We read many examples in the New Testament of this new role of the Holy Spirit (Acts 2:38, Acts 5:32, Acts 10:44). Throughout both the Old Testament and the New Testament we read of the Holy Spirit's work. It was after Jesus' death, however, that the Holy Spirit was given as a gift, a constant advocate, to everyone who is part of God's family.

Teaching 4: The Holy Spirit's Role in Salvation

Review Theme Verse

Since we live by the Spirit, let us keep in step with the Spirit. (Galatians 5:25)

DIGGING DOWN

Read this story about Johnny and Sam.

* * *

"I saw you steal that candy bar," declared Johnny to his twin brother Sam. Both boys stood in front of their mother, describing what had happened in the small corner store.

"No, I didn't steal it. The owner of the store gave it to me," retorted Sam as he explained why he was holding a candy bar that he had not paid for. Their mother was not sure what to do. Did Sam steal the candy bar, as Johnny stated, or did the owner give the candy bar to Sam as a gift? There was only one way to find out.

The two boys and their mother silently reentered the store, and she immediately asked to see the store owner. "My son says that you gave him this candy bar. Is that true?"

"Well, ma'am, it's like this," said the owner. "A few minutes ago both of your sons were in here and they knocked over a small display of baby diapers." He pointed to Johnny. "This boy immediately ran away. But this guy here," he pointed at Sam, "cleaned up the mess. When I saw that, I thought I should reward his helpfulness. Yes, ma'am, I did give him the candy bar."

After thanking the store owner for helping her know the truth, Sam's mom handed Sam the candy bar. "I am very glad we were able to talk to the owner. I now know that he gave you the candy bar and that you were telling the truth, Sam. Thank you."

* * *

In this story, Sam's mom needed to hear the truth not just from Sam, but also from the store owner. Often, if only one person tells what happens, we might doubt the truth of the story, but if two of the people involved give the same story, then we can believe that it is true.

Look Up and Read Romans 8:16

The Spirit himself testifies with our spirit that we are God's children.

We know that if we believe that Jesus paid for our sins, then we are part of God's family. However, do you ever doubt that you are part of God's family? This verse tells us we do not need to doubt that we are God's children because not just one person, but two of the people involved say it is true. Who are those two people?

The verse says that we are the first one. We believe that Jesus forgave our sins and that he can save us. The second person is the Holy Spirit. Because the Holy Spirit lives in us, the Spirit knows that we believe.

Doctrine of the Holy Spirit

The verse we read shows us that, whenever we doubt we are part of God's family, we can remember that we repented of our sin, and we believed Jesus paid for our sins. The Holy Spirit knows this is true. Because two people, the Holy Spirit and our self, know that we are God's children, we can believe it.

Questions

1. Why did Sam's mom believe that the store owner gave Sam the candy bar?

2. In the verse we read, Romans 8:16, how many people say that we are part of God's family?

3. What does the Holy Spirit know about us that helps him say that we are part of God's family?

Digging Deeper

Many countries in the world issue a birth certificate of some type when a child is born. In the United States, every baby born who is registered receives a certificate with a government seal on it, proving the certificate's authenticity. This seal is the official mark of the government, confirming that this child was born in the United States. If a birth certificate does not have the official seal, then the certificate is not considered legal.

> When God sets his seal on a man's heart by his Spirit, there is some holy stamp, some image impressed and left upon the heart by the Spirit, as by the seal upon the wax. And this holy stamp, or impressed image, exhibiting clear evidence to the conscience, that the subject of it is the child of God, is the very thing which in Scripture is called the seal of the Spirit.
> - *Jonathan Edwards* [2]

Did you know that the Holy Spirit was given to us as a seal?

Look Up and Read Ephesians 1:13-14

And you also were included in Christ when you heard the message of truth, the gospel of your salvation. When you believed, you were marked in him with a seal, the promised Holy Spirit, who is a deposit guaranteeing our inheritance until the redemption of those who are God's possession—to the praise of his glory.

Look Up and Read 2 Corinthians 1:21-22

Now it is God who makes both us and you stand firm in Christ. He anointed us, set his seal of ownership on us, and put his Spirit in our hearts as a deposit, guaranteeing what is to come.

God places the Holy Spirit on us as a seal, proving that we are authentic members of God's family. The Greek word translated as "seal" means, "To mark with a seal as a means of identification."[3] Just as a government puts a seal on a birth certificate to identify a child as being a member of its country, so God gives us a seal, the Holy Spirit, who identifies us as members of God's family.

Having the Holy Spirit with us as a seal not only identifies us as part of God's family right now, but it also guarantees that in the future we will inherit eternal life. It is as if God gives us the Holy Spirit as a down payment, assuring us that we have the hope of eternal life.

As soon as we receive the gift of forgiveness of sins, we receive the identification mark which is the seal, the Holy Spirit. The Holy Spirit, as a seal, identifies us as part of God's family, and he guarantees us the privileges that come with that position.

Although we often think of Jesus the Son as having the primary role in our salvation because he is the one who died and rose again, we actually see all three persons of the Trinity involved in saving us. God the Father planned our salvation (Eph. 1:4-5), Jesus the Son paid for it (1 Cor. 15:3-4), and the Holy Spirit is our guarantee and seal, identifying us as members in God's family. We can thank all three of them for their part in our salvation.

Teaching 5: The Holy Spirit Living in Us

Review Theme Verse

Since we live by the Spirit, let us keep in step with the Spirit. (Galatians 5:25)

DIGGING DOWN

At Christmastime, we usually give and receive gifts. Have you ever had a gift from someone that you just could not wait to open? You knew the giver had picked out something special, just for you, and you desperately wanted to know what it was! Presents are a wonderful way to show people that we love and appreciate them. When we give someone a present, we are telling them we think they are special! Did you know that God gave us a gift?

Look Up and Read Acts 2:38

Peter replied, "Repent and be baptized, every one of you, in the name of Jesus Christ for the forgiveness of your sins. And you will receive the gift of the Holy Spirit."

When we turn to God so our sins are forgiven, then we become part of God's family. But that is not all! When we become part of God's family, God gives us a special gift. God gives us the gift of the Holy Spirit!

The Holy Spirit then lives in us (2 Tim. 1:14). This does not mean that the Holy Spirit builds a house right between our lungs and stomach.

No, the Holy Spirit lives in our spirit so that he can help us, teach us, and guide us. As soon as we become part of God's family, God forgives us, and the Holy Spirit is given to us.

Sometimes when the Holy Spirit comes to live in a person, the person may feel different. In fact, when the Holy Spirit came to live in Jesus' friends, a loud noise sounded and flames of fire appeared over their heads (Acts 2:2-11). They all began speaking in languages that they did not know before! When they walked outside, talking in those languages, people who were visiting from all over the world recognized their language. This was how God immediately let people from all different nations know how wonderful God is and why they should believe in him. Jesus' friends could then tell everyone how to be part of God's family, and they could explain it in the language that each person best understood. Today, however, most people do not have such a dramatic display when they receive the gift of the Holy Spirit.

Although we do not have flames of fire over our heads when we receive the Holy Spirit, the Bible tells us that, when we are part of God's family, we do have this special gift from God. We do have the Holy Spirit now living in us, helping us, guiding us, and giving us courage. We can be sure that God loves us so much that he gives us this great gift.

Questions

1. What gift does God give us when we become part of his family?

2. What happened to Jesus' friends when they received the Holy Spirit?

3. What does the Holy Spirit want to do for you now that He is in you?

Digging Deeper

If you lived in the time of King Solomon, the third King of Israel, you would have seen a massive building project taking shape in Jerusalem. The temple of the Lord that Solomon built was not just a utilitarian building. Because Solomon understood that this building was where God would meet with people when they came to worship God, he insisted that it be an unblemished, magnificent structure. A hand-woven rich-colored curtain, pure gold decorative chains, gold bowls, and even gold covered walls and doors decorated this temple. The temple was Solomon's tribute to God. However, even though it was a majestic structure, this temple no longer stands.

Because the Israelites began worshipping idols, God allowed Jerusalem, along with the temple, to be destroyed. This spectacular temple that Solomon built no longer stands as a place where people can go to worship God. In fact, although the temple was rebuilt, it was later destroyed again. Today there is no temple in Jerusalem, but this does not mean that God no longer meets with us!

Look Up and Read 1 Corinthians 6:18-20

> *Flee from sexual immorality. All other sins a person commits are outside the body, but whoever sins sexually, sins against their own body. Do you not know that your bodies are temples of the Holy Spirit, who is in you, whom you have received from God? You are not your own; you were bought at a price. Therefore honor God with your bodies.*

These verses state that your body is the temple of the Holy Spirit. As a temple, your body is a place to worship God. Do you worship God with your body? Do you think the Holy Spirit is pleased with the temple that you are offering him?

Paul, the writer of 1 Corinthians, used the example of sexual immorality to show us how we can dishonor God with our body. When we engage in sexual practices with someone other than our spouse, we are using our body, the temple of the Holy Spirit, for sin. Therefore, we should be very careful what we look at and how we act because every time we sin with our body we are polluting the temple.

Solomon did not build a beautiful temple so that people could mock God by throwing mud at the walls and spitting on the floor. No, Solomon's temple was a magnificent, beautiful place so that everyone would know how great God is. This is how our bodies should be.

Jesus paid the price so that we can be part of God's family. God then gave us the Holy Spirit to help us. When we received the Holy Spirit, our bodies became the temple of God. By treating our bodies as the temple, we honor God and bring him fame. If we use our bodies for sin, we mock God and dishonor his name. "Therefore, I urge you, brothers and sisters, in view of God's mercy, to offer your bodies as a living sacrifice, holy and pleasing to God—this is your true and proper worship" (Rom. 12:1).

Teaching 6: The Holy Spirit Helps Us

Review Theme Verse

Since we live by the Spirit, let us keep in step with the Spirit. (Galatians 5:25)

Digging Down

You can either choose one person to do this activity while everyone watches, or have everyone participate. First, get a piece of paper and a pen or pencil for each person participating. Now, close your eyes and draw a picture of your family. When you are done, look at your picture. That drawing probably does not look much like your family! Are the ears and eyes in the wrong place (are they even on the head)? Are the legs connected to the bodies?

Now, close your eyes again. This time have someone, with their eyes open, hold onto your hand to help you draw your family. When you are done, look at the picture the two of you drew together. It probably looks much better than the first picture because you received help from someone who could see.

Although you will not go through life with your eyes closed, there will be many times in your life when it feels like you cannot see what to do next. You may be sad, lonely, discouraged, or feeling like you will never be able to learn or do the things you should. Perhaps there is a project you need to do or a person you need to forgive. These are hard to do, and just as we could not draw the picture without help, we also need help to accomplish these things. Did you know that the Holy Spirit helps us?

Look Up and Read Romans 8:26

> *In the same way, the Spirit helps us in our weakness. We do not know what we ought to pray for, but the Spirit himself intercedes for us through wordless groans.*

This verse states that the Holy Spirit helps us in our weakness. That means that the Holy Spirit, who lives in us, will always help us! When we feel sad, angry, or discouraged, the Holy Spirit helps us pray. The Holy Spirit also gives us hope (Rom. 15:13).

Another way that the Holy Spirit helps us is by teaching us. He teaches us how much Jesus loves us (Eph. 3:16-19) as well as what is true about

God (1 Cor. 2:11-12). In fact, if we didn't have the Holy Spirit, we could not understand the Bible (1 Cor. 2:13-14).

The Holy Spirit also helps us say and do what God would want us to say and do (Luke 12:11-12). It is wonderful that we have God the Holy Spirit always with us to help us!

There are times when we do not know how to forgive or help someone. We want to but it is as if our eyes are closed and we are stumbling around, unable to see. Or, it might feel like we have no hope because a situation seems too hard. It is as if we are drawing a picture in the dark. The Holy Spirit can help us during these times because the Holy Spirit is God. With God (who sees and knows everything) helping us, we will know what to say and do. We can then have hope. With the Holy Spirit's help, the picture of our lives will turn out beautifully!

Questions

1. Who is always with us to help us?
2. What are some ways that the Holy Spirit helps us?

Digging Deeper

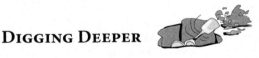

When an item is invented, the inventor knows what its purpose is. For instance, the inventor of the chair expected people to sit on it. The inventor did not suggest that someone try to fry an egg on the chair or cure a disease with the chair. The chair was invented for people to sit on. This seems like common sense. In fact, if you received a chair as a birthday gift and you tried to dribble it like a basketball, you would be very disappointed. That gift was not meant to be used as a basketball. The chair was meant to sit on. Although we understand the purpose for most gifts we receive, including a chair, sometimes we become confused about the purpose of the gifts that God gives us.

The Holy Spirit gives us gifts (1 Cor. 12:11). Romans 12: 6-8 mentions some of the gifts, including the gift of prophecy, the gift of serving, the gift of teaching, the gift of encouraging, the gift of giving, the gift of leading, and the gift of showing mercy. We all have gifts that the Holy Spirit has given us, but do we understand the purpose of those gifts? There are two purposes mentioned in the following scripture. What are they?

Look Up and Read 1 Peter 4:10-11

> *Each of you should use whatever gift you have received to serve others, as faithful stewards of God's grace in its various forms. If anyone speaks, they should do so as one who speaks the very words of God. If anyone serves, they should do so with the strength God provides, so that in all things God may be praised through Jesus Christ. To him be the glory and the power for ever and ever. Amen.*

The first purpose is to "serve others." God has given us gifts which we should use to serve others. This is very difficult! For instance, if you have the gift of leadership, it could be tempting to use this gift to make yourself look good. You might try to prove how right you are or attempt to make people serve you. Instead, this gift should be used to help those around you. This would be done by leading well, by looking out for the interests of others.

Perhaps you have the gift of teaching and you are able to give an incredible lesson. Should you use that gift to make yourself look great? No, it should be used to help others understand the information taught. You are, then, serving your students. Whatever gifts we have we should use to serve others.

The second purpose for the gifts the Holy Spirit gives us is so that God would be praised (v. 11). Whatever gift you have, whether it is serving, encouraging, teaching, leading, or one of the other gifts, you must use that gift so that God would be praised. Again, this is a difficult purpose! Often we use our gifts so that we look good, but this is not the purpose of the gift. It is like trying to dribble a chair. It's the wrong purpose, and it won't work very well for long. Instead, when we teach it should be so that God becomes famous. We should lead so that God gets the credit. We should encourage others not just to help others, but so that God gets praised.

Every gift from the Holy Spirit is given for these two purposes: to serve others and so that God gets praised. When we use our gifts with these purposes, as they were intended to be used, we will be glorifying God and making him famous. Think about what gifts the Holy Spirit has given you. Are you using them to serve others and to give God praise? If not, then you are dribbling a chair.

DOCTRINE OF PEOPLE

Overview

Do you belong to someone? If you are held captive or living in slavery, you may be told that you belong to the one who enslaves you. Some governments may say that you belong to them, and your job may require so much of your time and energy that it feels as though you belong to it. There are people who balk at the idea of belonging to anyone; these people believe that they only belong to themselves. Our question remains, "Do *you* belong to someone?"

Our theme verse for the Doctrine of People assures us that we belong to God. "Know that the LORD is God. It is he who made us, and we are his; we are his people, the sheep of his pasture" (Ps. 100:3).

Know that the LORD is God. The NET Bible[1] translates this scripture as, "Realize that the LORD is God!" Know. Realize. Be assured. The Lord is God. Not "a" god, but capital "G" God. In other words, the Lord of the Bible is the creative, powerful being behind our existence and the existence of all creation.

It is he who made us, and we are his; we are his people, the sheep of his pasture. If the Lord is God, then we must understand that we all belong to him. Just as sheep belong to the shepherd, so all of creation belongs to its creator. This means that, contrary to popular belief, we do not belong to ourselves nor do we belong to another human being. We belong to our creator; we belong to God. Thankfully, God is not a vicious, ego-maniac who desires to hurt us. Psalm 100 gives a few of God's characteristics. These assure us that belonging to God is not a burden but a joy.

For the LORD is good (Ps. 100:5a). Because God is good, he desires to help us and provide for us just as a shepherd helps and provides for his sheep. God does not desire to destroy us or hurt us because God is good.

His love endures forever (Ps. 100:5b). God's love for us goes beyond just a fleeting feeling of affection. He loves us with a loyal love that will not wane or falter. (The NET Bible[2] translates this "His loyal love endures.") Unlike people whose love fluctuates, God's love remains loyal and steadfast.

His faithfulness continues through all generations (Ps.100:5c). Just as God's love does not change with time, neither does his faithfulness. God's love, provision, and help will be given to us just as it was given to previous generations and will be given to our children and beyond.

God is good, God has loyal love for us, and God is faithful to us. These are some reasons why we love, worship, and serve our amazing creator—God. Psalm 100 shows what our response should be to knowing that we belong to such a wonderful God.

Look Up and Read Psalm 100

> *Shout for joy to the LORD, all the earth. Worship the LORD with gladness; come before him with joyful songs. Know that the LORD is God. It is he who made us, and we are his, we are his people, the sheep of his pasture. Enter his gates with thanksgiving and his courts with praise; give thanks to him and praise his name. For the LORD is*

good and his love endures forever; his faithfulness continues through all generations.

Theme Verse for Memorization: Psalm 100:3

Know that the LORD is God. It is he who made us, and we are his; we are his people, the sheep of his pasture.

Let's learn who we, as people, are.

Teaching 1: People Were Created to Glorify God

Review Theme Verse

Know that the LORD is God. It is he who made us, and we are his; we are his people, the sheep of his pasture. (Psalm 100:3)

DIGGING DOWN

Have you ever seen any of the Olympic Games? Countries around the world send their best athletes to these games to compete against each other in a variety of sports such as skiing, kayaking, and soccer. The athletes, whether on skis, in a boat, or kicking a ball, compete not just for themselves but for their country.

Since these athletes compete as representatives of their country, we say that "The United States got a silver medal" or "Russia got the gold medal" even though it was the athlete who competed in the sport, not the entire country! In other words, these athletes, as representatives of their countries, can make a country proud or, if they act badly, they make their country ashamed. If they win, their country looks good! Although most of us will never compete in the Olympic Games, did you know that we are also representatives?

When we are Christians and are part of God's family, then we represent God. In other words, when people see us help someone, people will say, "Wow, people who follow Jesus are kind." But, when we hurt someone, people will say, "People who believe in Jesus are mean." What we do can help make Jesus famous or will turn people away from wanting to follow Jesus.

Just as Olympic athletes represent their countries to the world, we represent Jesus to the world. Therefore we should make sure that everything we do and say makes Jesus proud.

Look Up and Read Colossians 3:17

> *And whatever you do, whether in word or deed, do it all in the name of the Lord Jesus, giving thanks to God the Father through him.*

This verse says that everything we do or say should be done in the name of Jesus. This means that we are Jesus' representatives.[3] As his representatives, we must choose to act how Jesus wants us to act and say only the things that Jesus would want us to say. We should be kind, not mean (Eph. 4:32). We should tell the truth, not lie (Col. 3:9). We should obey our parents, not disobey them (Eph. 6:1). When we act as Jesus wants us to act, we make him famous.

Isaiah, a prophet we read about in the Old Testament, prayed, "We desire your fame and reputation to grow" (Isa. 26:8b NET).[4] We too can pray that God's fame and reputation continue to grow. It is our job, as part of God's family, to use our words and our actions to make God famous because we are his representatives.

Questions

1. Just as Olympic athletes represent their countries, we represent someone. Who do we represent?
2. As God's representatives, what should be our goal?

3. What are ways we can act or things we can say that would not make God famous?

4. What are ways we can act or things we can say that would make God famous?

Digging Deeper

Imagine that you are a distinguished potter, one who is world-renowned because of the exquisite masterpieces you create. One day, as you sit down to begin your next project, the lump of clay looks up at you from the pottery wheel and exclaims, "Oh, I do hope that you are going to make me into a beautiful vase that will be admired in the national museum." "Well," you reply, "I actually was going to make you into a bowl because our dog needs a new water dish." "A dog's water dish? Are you kidding me?" gasps the lump of clay, "I need to be important and admired. I need fame and fortune. I will not allow myself to become a common water dish for you. I have my own plans for my life." With that, the lump jumps off the pottery wheel and begins rolling toward the door.

This scene seems pretty silly, doesn't it? Obviously lumps of clay cannot talk, nor can they decide what they want to be or where they want to be placed. All of those decisions are the potter's, and the lump must be formed and fashioned under the potter's skilled hands. In fact, even if the lump was made into a beautiful vase that was placed in the national museum, it is not the vase that becomes famous, but the potter who created the vase. There are many instances in the Bible where God is compared to a potter and people are like the lump of clay.

The prophet Isaiah makes this comparison as he states, "Yet you, LORD, are our Father. We are the clay, you are the potter; we are all the work of your hand" (Isa. 64:8). We are God's creation, just as a vase or a dog's water dish is the potter's creation, and it is ridiculous to think that we can demand that the potter obey our wishes and always give us exactly what we want.

Look Up and Read Isaiah 29:16

> *You turn things upside down, as if the potter were thought to be like the clay! Shall what is formed say to the one who formed it, "You did not make me"? Can the pot say to the potter, "You know nothing"?*

Here Isaiah again uses the image of a potter and pot to show how silly it is for people to think that they are independent of God. As the potter, God does know each one of us. God made us, and God understands everything about our lives, including what he would like us to do and be. This means that God knows how to help us, love us, and provide for us far better than we could ever do for ourselves! Too often, even though we are the created pots, we approach our relationship with God thinking that we know what is best for our lives. This means that we expect God to fulfill our desires and demands. If he doesn't, then we get upset with God.

This problem of a me-centered relationship with God is not new. Malachi, the last Old Testament prophet, writes a condemnation of some of the Jews. What was their sin? They were turning away from God because they felt they did not gain anything from the relationship.

Look Up and Read Malachi 3:14-18

> *"You have said, 'It is futile to serve God. What do we gain by carrying out his requirements and going about like mourners before the LORD Almighty? But now we call the arrogant blessed. Certainly evildoers prosper, and even when they put God to the test, they get away with it.'" Then those who feared the LORD talked with each*

other, and the LORD listened and heard. A scroll of remembrance was written in his presence concerning those who feared the LORD and honored his name. "On the day when I act," says the LORD Almighty, "they will be my treasured possession. I will spare them, just as a father has compassion and spares his son who serves him. And you will again see the distinction between the righteous and the wicked, between those who serve God and those who do not."

These verses tell the story of two different groups of people. The me-centered group weighed their sacrifices for God against what they wanted God to do for them. "What do we gain?" they asked (v. 14). They concluded that following God did not give them what they wanted so they deserted him. The other group realized their arrogance, and God assured them that, because he loved them as a father loves his children, he would have compassion on them and help them.

So, how do we have a God-centered attitude instead of a me-centered one? We must realize that God is our creator; he is the potter. As our creator, God immensely loves us. He also demands and deserves our love, respect, and obedience. As the created pot, we should look at our lives from God's perspective, not our own. We should love and serve God, not demand that God obey us. We should make the potter famous.

Teaching 2: People Sin

Review Theme Verse

Know that the LORD is God. It is he who made us, and we are his; we are his people, the sheep of his pasture. (Psalm 100:3)

Digging Down

What is your favorite subject in school? Perhaps it is history, math, or writing. Each of these subjects helps us learn more about our world and how to live in it. Interestingly, there are some subjects that are not taught in school. For instance, have you ever taken a class called "How to Cheat on your Test," or "How to be Mean to your Sister"? Has your teacher ever told you to read a book named *How to Lie*? Chances are you have not been in a class or read a book that teaches you those things. And yet, it is very likely that you have cheated, been mean, or lied. If you were not taught how to do these things, then how do you know how to do them?

Each of those actions: cheating, lying, and being mean are sin. Sin means to disobey God, and people do not need to be taught how to disobey God because people are born as sinners.

Look Up and Read Psalm 51:5

Surely I was sinful at birth, sinful from the time my mother conceived me.

King David stated that he was a sinner when he was born. When he wrote this verse, was King David telling us that while his mother was pregnant he snuck out of his mother's womb, robbed a bank, and then snuck back in? Obviously not! King David was admitting that all people, himself included, are born sinners. We do not need to be taught how to sin. We already know how. All people are born with what is called original sin. This means that all people are born sinners. How did people get to have original sin?

All humans have sin because Adam, who was the first person created, sinned (Rom. 5:12, 1 Cor. 15:21-22).

All people came from Adam. As a result, all people inherited Adam's physical traits such as eyes, ears, and toes. All people also inherited the spiritual trait of sin from Adam. Adam sinned so we all are born with sin just as we are born with eyes, ears, and toes. No one, except Jesus, is born perfect. (Jesus, because he was fully God as well as being fully human, never sinned. He is the only human being who has never sinned.) Everyone is born a sinner; everyone has original sin.

Because we are born sinners, we do not need to be taught how to sin. Lying, cheating, and being mean are a natural part of who we are. However, we should not think that it is okay to sin just because we have original sin. Instead of using original sin as an excuse to continue to sin, we must turn away from our sin and try to follow God with our actions and attitudes.

Look Up and Read Colossians 3:8-10

> *But now you must also rid yourselves of all such things as these: anger, rage, malice, slander, and filthy language from your lips. Do not lie to each other, since you have taken off your old self with its practices and have put on the new self, which is being renewed in knowledge in the image of its Creator.*

Being angry, lying, and being mean are easy for people to do because of original sin. However, these verses state that we must "take off" these things. Just as we take off dirty socks and put on clean ones, we must take off our sinful actions and put on actions that make God famous.

Questions

1. Why do we not need to take a class that teaches us how to cheat or lie?

2. What does "sin" mean?

3. What does "original sin" mean?

4. What are some physical characteristics that people have because they came from Adam? What is a spiritual characteristic?

Digging Deeper

If you were to stand in front of God and tell him why you think you should get into heaven, what would you say? Many people, if given that scenario, would state that they would tell God that they have been good, kind, and that they even helped a little old lady who was crossing the street. However, we have to ask, "Are any of us good enough to convince God that we should get into heaven because of our own merit?" The answer to that question is an emphatic, "No!"

> This, then, is what it means to begin true repentance; and here man must hear such a sentence as this: You are all of no account, whether you be manifest sinners or saints (in your own opinion); you all must become different and do otherwise than you now are and are doing (no matter what sort of people you are), whether you are as great, wise, powerful, and holy as you may. Here no one is (righteous, holy), godly, etc.
> - Martin Luther[5]

For example, we all have original sin. We are born sinners. However, we cannot get upset with Adam for our sin because we also willfully sin. This means that each one of us actually chooses to sin; we choose to disobey God. How can we tell if we have sinned?

Look Up and Read Romans 3:20

> *Therefore no one will be declared righteous in God's sight by the works of the law; rather, through the law we become conscious of our sin.*

What is the guide we can use? Romans 3:20 states that we become aware of sin by examining God's laws.

Exodus 20 outlines some of the law. "You shall not murder" is one of God's laws (v. 13). You may never have killed someone, but Jesus expanded the definition of murder as he stated, "You have heard that it was said to the people long ago, 'You shall not murder, and anyone who murders will be subject to judgment.' But I tell you that anyone who is angry with a brother or sister will be subject to judgment" (Matt. 5:21-22a). Therefore, if you have ever been wrongfully angry with someone, then you have disobeyed God.

Another law given in Exodus 20 is "You shall not commit adultery" (v. 14). Although you may never have had a physical relationship with someone who is not your spouse, you still could have committed adultery because Jesus expanded the meaning of adultery. He stated, "You have heard that it was said, 'You shall not commit adultery.' But I tell you that anyone who looks at a woman lustfully has already committed adultery with her in his heart" (Matt. 5:27-28).

These are just two of the laws, and probably there is not one person on the planet who has obeyed both of these! Obviously we cannot blame all of our sin on Adam. We all choose to sin, and each of us must pay for our disobedience to God. Our good deeds cannot cancel the punishment that we must receive because of our sin.

Think again of the scenario of standing before God, trying to convince him that you should be allowed into Heaven because of your own goodness. Even the most kind, generous, loving person has disobeyed God by breaking the law. Because our good does not cancel out our sin, we cannot earn a spot in God's kingdom.

Teaching 3: The Necessary Decision

Review Theme Verse

Know that the LORD is God. It is he who made us, and we are his; we are his people, the sheep of his pasture. (Psalm 100:3)

Digging Down

Everyone stand up and walk straight forward. Now, change your mind about which direction to walk, and walk in a different direction. Then, come back and sit down.

Just as you changed your mind about which direction to walk, there are many times when we make a decision and then change our minds. For instance, if you could choose a snack to eat, you might first think that a banana sounds good. But, when you see some fresh-baked cookies, you change your mind and choose a cookie. Or perhaps when you got dressed this morning you first picked out one shirt then changed your mind and chose a different one. We probably all change our minds about something every day, and most of these decisions do not radically change our lives. It usually does not matter which shirt we wear or what exact snack we eat today. These are small decisions that we make. However, there is one big decision that every person, at some point in their lives, must make.

This decision involves us changing our minds about our sin. When we are born we have original sin, and as we grow we continue to choose to sin. It is as if we are walking straight toward sin, but we don't even know that it is wrong. However, God says that sin *is* wrong, and we must not think that it is alright to sin. Instead, we must change our mind about sin and choose to stop disobeying him; we must choose to walk toward God, away from sin.

Doctrine of People

Look Up and Read Acts 20:21

I have declared to both Jews and Greeks that they must turn to God in repentance and have faith in our Lord Jesus.

In this verse we read how Paul, a famous preacher, summed up everything he taught people. He said that people needed to "turn to God in repentance." Repentance in the Bible means to change our mind. So when we repent of our sin, we are changing our mind about our sin. We are agreeing with God that our sin is wrong.

In order to become part of God's family, every person must change his or her mind about the sin that is done and choose to walk away from that sin and turn to walk toward God. This does not mean that a person in God's family will never sin, but it does mean that a person must understand that sinning is wrong.

Paul also taught that, in order to be part of God's family, one must "have faith in our Lord Jesus." We must believe that Jesus died and rose again and depend on Jesus' death and resurrection to forgive our sins.[6] When we have faith that Jesus forgives our sins, then we become part of his family.

As we learned in previous lessons, God planned our salvation, Jesus paid for our salvation, and the Holy Spirit assures us that we are saved.[7] Our responsibility in becoming part of God's family is to repent of our sin and to have faith in Jesus. The decision to repent and have faith is necessary for us to be part of God's family.

Questions

1. What does sin mean?
2. What does repentance mean?
3. What does it mean to change our mind about our sin?
4. What do we need to do in order to become part of God's family?

Digging Deeper

Each person on this planet lives a set of unique events. For instance, some people are from large families, some from small. Some have read many books, others have read few. Some have visited other countries, others have not. There is no one else on this earth who is living the exact life that you are living. However, even though we all have different lives, we all face the same end. We all will die.

There are many different theories about what happens to people after they die. Some people believe in reincarnation. This theory states that after you die you will be born back on this earth in a different form. If you were good in your previous life, you may come back as a prince. However, if you were bad in your previous life, then you may come back as a cockroach. You can learn the Bible's response to reincarnation in Hebrews.

Look Up and Read Hebrews 9:27-28

> *Just as people are destined to die once, and after that to face judgment, so Christ was sacrificed once to take away the sins of many; and he will appear a second time, not to bear sin, but to bring salvation to those who are waiting for him.*

This verse states that each person will die once – not over and over and over – and then will face judgment.

Other people believe that there is nothing after you die. In other words, we live on this earth, and then we cease to exist. Paul wrote a lengthy argument to show that we do not cease to exist after we die (1 Cor. 15:12-58). Instead, we are resurrected, given new bodies, and will live eternally. At the end of his argument, he asked, "Where, O death, is your victory? Where, O death, is your sting?" (v. 55). Death is not the end; death is not victorious over our lives. We will continue living forever.

Interestingly, some people falsely believe that, after we die, we will become angels. Although our eternal bodies will be different from our earthly bodies (1 Cor. 15:53), we do not actually change into a different being. We will continue being human, and humans are a different type of being than angels.

Another popular belief is that, because God exercises perfect love, he will allow all people to be with him after they die. Although we know that God is love, we also know that God is just. It is God's justice that declares there will be a judgment, and only those who are part of his family will be allowed to spend eternity with him.

Imagine that a thief came into your home and killed your entire family, leaving you as the sole survivor. Entering the courtroom where this thief-turned-murderer is on trial, you hear people murmuring. Straining your ears to hear, you catch phrases such as, "He is so loving," and, "This judge is the nicest judge." The whispering stops as the court is called to order. After all of the incontestable evidence is given, the judge stands up and faces the courtroom. "Well," he begins, "Obviously there is irrefutable evidence proving the guilt of this man. However, I really love people, and I just can't make myself condemn him."

Instead of insisting that there must be punishment for this crime, the judge puts aside his responsibility to be just. None of us would want that type of judge trying this case.

Because God is just, he must insist that there be punishment for our sin-crime. Thankfully, Jesus offered to pay the penalty for our sin with his blood (Rev. 1:5). When we acknowledge that Jesus' blood paid the penalty for our sin and that he carried our sin away, then we can live for eternity with God unpunished. This is why the decision of repenting from our own sin and admitting that we need Jesus to pay for our sin is the most important decision that we will ever make. Only when you depend on Jesus to save you from the penalty of your sins will you know for sure what will happen to you after you die.

Teaching 4: God's Commands for People

Review Theme Verse

Know that the LORD is God. It is he who made us, and we are his; we are his people, the sheep of his pasture. (Psalm 100:3)

DIGGING DOWN

Every family and school has rules. Name one rule that you have in your life. Perhaps you mentioned brushing your teeth, doing your homework, or not hitting someone. There are many different rules that people must obey. God also has rules that we, as part of his family, must live by.

Two thousand years ago, when Jesus lived on earth, there were 613 rules that the Jews thought that they needed to obey in order to please God.[8] Some were as basic as "Do not believe in any other God," but there were other rules such as "A leper must shave his head" and "Do not shave your beard."[9]

There was a group of people who knew all 613 laws, and they tried to make sure everyone obeyed them. One of these experts in the law asked Jesus what the most important command was.

Look Up and Read Matthew 22:35-38

> *One of them, an expert in the law, tested him with this question: "Teacher, which is the greatest commandment in the Law?" Jesus replied: "'Love the Lord your God with all your heart and with all your soul and with all your mind.' This is the first and greatest commandment."*

Jesus said that the primary rule, or command, that people should follow is, "Love the Lord your God with all your heart and with all your soul and with all your mind."[10] When you love someone, you have joy being with that person. You also work hard to spend time with that person, and you keep that person as the highest priority in your life. It is the same with God. When we love God we have joy spending time with him, and we choose to make God the highest priority in our lives. By including three parts of a person, the heart, the soul, and the mind, Jesus stated that a person must completely and fully love God.[11] In other words, a person's thoughts, actions, and attitudes must all show love for God.

Often we say that we love God, but our actions do not show it. For instance, which would you want to attend, church or a sports game? Do you spend time reading the Bible, or do you only read other books and magazines? Do you think that your friends can tell that you love God, or would they say that something else is more important to you than God?

Your attitude should also show your love for God. Do you enjoy spending time with God as you read the Bible? Do you look forward to spending time with other Christians? Are you kind, loving, and forgiving, or do you get angry and hold grudges? Do you thank God for everything that he has done for you? Do you sing songs about how amazing God is?

These are suggestions to help us think about whether we truly do love God and have God first in our lives. There is no official list of rules that we need to keep to prove that we love God. Instead, we must be aware that all of our attitudes and actions should show that we do truly love God with all of our hearts, souls, and minds.

Questions

1. According to Jesus, what is the greatest command in the Bible?

2. When Jesus says that we must love God with our heart, soul, and mind, what does he mean?

3. What are ways that we can show that we truly love God?

Digging Deeper

According to Jesus, the first and greatest command that his followers must obey is to "Love the Lord your God with all your heart and with all your soul and with all your mind" (Matt. 22:37). However, Jesus did not stop there. The second greatest command tells us that we must also love other people. "Love your neighbor as yourself," stated Jesus. (Matt. 22:39b). He then clarified that a neighbor is anyone to whom we can show mercy (Luke 10:36-37). In other words, the second greatest command for us to obey is to show kindness, love, and mercy to everyone around us, regardless of what they can do for us. We see this command conveyed throughout the Bible.

Although the Old Testament law required the Israelites to treat the poor and the rich equally (Lev. 19:15), that did not always happen. Repeatedly we read of God's judgment on the Jews because they exploited the poor, crushing them in their stampede for wealth. Two prophets who spoke out against the Jews' lack of mercy for the poor were Ezekiel and Amos.

Look Up and Read Ezekiel 22:29

The people of the land practice extortion and commit robbery; they oppress the poor and needy and mistreat the foreigner, denying them justice.

Look Up and Read Amos 5:11-12

You levy a straw tax on the poor and impose a tax on their grain. Therefore, though you have built stone mansions, you will not live in them; though you have planted lush vineyards, you will not drink their wine. For I know how many are your offenses and how great your sins. There are those who oppress the innocent and take bribes and deprive the poor of justice in the courts.

God's command for people to show mercy and justice is repeated in the New Testament.

Look Up and Read James 2:1-4

My brothers and sisters, believers in our glorious Lord Jesus Christ must not show favoritism. Suppose a man comes into your meeting wearing a gold ring and fine clothes, and a poor man in filthy old clothes also comes in. If you show special attention to the man wearing fine clothes and say, "Here's a good seat for you," but say to the poor man, "You stand there" or "Sit on the floor by my feet," have you not discriminated among yourselves and become judges with evil thoughts?

Here we are explicitly warned not to show favoritism to the rich. In fact, the verse right before these says, "Religion that God our Father accepts as pure and faultless is this: to look after orphans and widows in their distress and to keep oneself from being polluted by the world" (James 1:27).

In Bible times, the male provided the income for a family. If a woman was widowed or children were orphaned, then they were extremely poor. Unfortunately, they often had no way of getting jobs or creating income. They needed someone to help them. James wrote that, if we overlook the poor around us, then God will not accept our religion as pure. We must show mercy and love to those who may not be able to repay us. We must love our neighbor as we love ourselves. James makes it clear that if we say we are religious but ignore or, even worse, exploit, the poor, then God considers our religion worthless.

Often it is easier to sit around a table, talking about Jesus, than to help the poor. However, James gives a warning in James 2:14-16. If we seek to meet someone's spiritual need while ignoring their physical need, then our faith is worthless. These are strong warnings: Be aware of those in need around you. Do not exploit the poor; seek justice. Try to help those in need. This is not an easy task, but the Bible shows us that God's desire is for us to treat all human beings as his creation, deserving justice and kindness.

As we show mercy and kindness to everyone around us, including the poor who will not be able to repay us, then we will be living the second greatest commandment, "Love your neighbor as yourself" (Matt. 22:39b).

Teaching 5: The Ultimate Charge

Review Theme Verse

Know that the LORD is God. It is he who made us, and we are his; we are his people, the sheep of his pasture. (Psalm 100:3)

DIGGING DOWN

In what country do you live? Would you say that most people living in your country believe in Jesus and obey God's words in the Bible? Do you know anyone who does not believe in Jesus? Most of us probably know someone who does not believe. The Bible tells us what Jesus wants us to do about that.

Look Up and Read Matthew 28:18-20

> *Then Jesus came to them and said, "All authority in heaven and on earth has been given to me. Therefore go and make disciples of all nations, baptizing them in the name of the Father and of the Son and of the Holy Spirit, and teaching them to obey everything I have commanded you. And surely I am with you always, to the very end of the age."*

These are some of the last words that Jesus said to his friends before he went back to heaven. What was his command? "Go and make disciples of all nations" (v. 19a). To be a disciple means to follow Jesus, to obey him, and to want to learn from him. We become a disciple when we enter God's family. Jesus wants everyone, from every country, to become his disciple.

How do we carry out this command? Think about how you learned of Jesus. Did your parents or someone at your church tell you about him? If no one had told you about Jesus, would you know about him? Just as someone needed to tell us about Jesus, so we need to tell others about Jesus. When we do that, we are making disciples, just as Jesus wanted.

There may be people around you who do not know Jesus. You can first pray for them and then tell them about Jesus. There are also people in other countries who do not know about Jesus. As a young person, you may not be able to go to a different country to tell people about Jesus, but you can pray for people from these countries. You can pray that an adult will go and tell them about Jesus. You can also ask God if he wants you, when you become an adult, to go to a different country or a different area of your country to tell people about Jesus.

The Bible tells us of Jesus' last instructions to his friends. One of the instructions was that they should go and make disciples. That is our job too.

Questions

1. What did Jesus command his friends to do?

2. Is there someone you know whom you want to pray for? Perhaps as a family you could make a list of people to pray for.

3. Will you pray and ask Jesus to make you willing to go anywhere in the world to teach others about God?

Digging Deeper

In the Bible there are numerous examples of one person telling another person about who God is so that the person will love and worship God. The Israelite Jonah traveled to Nineveh, the capital city of Assyria, which was an enemy of Israel. As Jonah preached about the upcoming destruction that God would cause, the people of Nineveh believed God and repented of their sin (Jon. 3:5, 10).

A Jewish slave girl, who had been captured and taken to the country of Aram, shared her faith with her master, Naaman. She encouraged him to seek God's help with his leprosy (2 Kings 5:3). Because of this young girl's determination to tell him of God's power, Naaman, a high official in Aram's army, was healed. As a result he declared, "Now I know that there is no God in all the world except in Israel" (2 Kings 5:15b).

Philip, as he spoke to an Ethiopian man, shared his faith with this foreigner. The Ethiopian believed in Jesus and became part of God's family (Acts 8:35). The Bible is full of examples and declarations of how God desires that people from every culture and language love and worship him. Has this happened?

Out of the 6.75 billion people in the world, 2.80 billion people are part of an "unreached" people group.[12] This means that 2.80 billion people in the world have no Bible, no church, and no way to hear about Jesus. Put another way, there are 16,595 people groups in the world, and 6,872 of them are unreached.[13] 41.4 percent of the people groups in the world do not have the choice to become part of God's family because they have no way of knowing who Jesus is.[14] Jesus wants everyone to worship him, and yet there are billions of people who have not even heard about him!

Look Up and Read Romans 10:9-15

> *If you declare with your mouth, "Jesus is Lord," and believe in your heart that God raised him from the dead, you will be saved. For it is with your heart that you believe and are justified, and it is with your mouth that you profess your faith and are saved. As Scripture says, "Anyone who believes in him will never be put to shame." For there is no difference between Jew and Gentile—the same Lord is Lord of all and richly blesses all who call on him, for, "Everyone who calls on the name of the Lord will be saved." How, then, can they call on the one they have not believed in? And how can they believe in the one of whom they have not heard? And how can they hear without someone preaching to them? And how can anyone preach unless they are sent? As it is written: "How beautiful are the feet of those who bring good news!"*

In order for people to believe in Jesus, they must hear about him. In order for them to hear about him, someone must go to them and tell them. It is very simple. 41.4 percent of the world's population has no way of deciding whether they want to be part of God's family or not because no one has gone to tell them that they have this choice![15] Whose responsibility is it to tell the unreached?

Handing It Down

It is ours. Perhaps we will be like Jonah and actually travel to a different country; perhaps we will be like Naaman's slave girl or Philip where God will bring someone to us. Or perhaps God has called us to use our finances to help those who do go.

Look Up and Read Psalm 67

> *May God be gracious to us and bless us and make his face shine on us—so that your ways may be known on earth, your salvation among all nations. May the peoples praise you, God; may all the peoples praise you. May the nations be glad and sing for joy, for you rule the peoples with equity and guide the nations of the earth. May the peoples praise you, God; may all the peoples praise you. The land yields its harvest; God, our God, blesses us. May God bless us still, so that all the ends of the earth will fear him.*

Notice that the prayer is for God to bless us "*so that* your ways may be known on earth, your salvation among all nations" (emphasis mine). God has blessed many of us with finances, education, health, and talents, and we must use those resources to share salvation with the people from every nation. Having the gift of salvation, we should be willing to share that gift with the world.

FAMILY FUN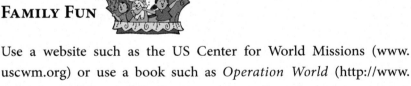

Use a website such as the US Center for World Missions (www.uscwm.org) or use a book such as *Operation World* (http://www.operationworld.org) to look up a country where there are not many Christians. Research that country and make a prayer card that you will keep somewhere where you spend time together as a family, such as at the dinner table. Decide to pray together that the people from that country would hear about Jesus.

Teaching 6: What Do People Get NOW?

Review Theme Verse

Know that the LORD is God. It is he who made us, and we are his; we are his people, the sheep of his pasture. (Psalm 100:3)

Digging Down

What is the best gift that you have received? Do you remember who it was from? Perhaps it was wrapped in pretty paper and given on a special occasion. Maybe it was a simple gift such as your father making you a sandwich or your mother fixing your toy. These are all gifts given to us because someone loves us.

Just as your father, mother, grandmother, or teacher may express their love by giving you special gifts, so also God gives us special gifts. They are not always wrapped in pretty paper and given on a special occasion. Most gifts are everyday gifts such as getting enough to eat or having time to play. However, they are all gifts, and they all come from God.

Look Up and Read Matthew 7:9-11

Which of you, if your son asks for bread, will give him a stone? Or if he asks for a fish, will give him a snake? If you, then, though you are evil, know how to give good gifts to your children, how much more will your Father in heaven give good gifts to those who ask him!

Have you ever eagerly ripped the wrapping paper off of a present only to find that the box contained a dirty rock? Or, were you ever hungry, and when you asked your parent for a snack, instead they handed you a snake? Of course not!

In these verses, Jesus taught that, just as a father loves giving good gifts to his child, so God the Father loves giving good gifts to us. Notice that Jesus said God will give "good gifts" (v. 11). This does not mean God will give us every toy that we ask him for, but he will give us everything that he thinks is best for us. He gives us good gifts.

We do not need to think, however, that God will only give us practical items such as socks and underwear. God gives us many things to enjoy as well. In fact, 1 Timothy 6:17b says, "Put [your] hope in God, who richly provides us with everything for our enjoyment." God gives us things, including our toys, family, flowers, and food, so that we can enjoy them. God loves it when we get joy from what he gives us.

Sometimes people, when they become part of God's family, only look at the future gift of living forever with God. Although we will receive that wonderful gift, we also receive many gifts here on earth. We can pray and ask God our Father for anything, and, if it is a gift that God thinks would be best for us, then he will give it to us. Isn't that wonderful? We have the creator of the universe, the all-powerful, all-wise God as our Father, and he loves giving us good gifts!

The Apostle Paul, in a letter to remind people of God's love for them, wrote, "If God is for us, who can be against us? He who did not spare his own Son, but gave him up for us all—how will he not also, along with him, graciously give us all things?" (Rom. 8:31b-32). God sent his own Son to die so Jesus could forgive our sins. Since God has that much love for us, he must love us enough to give us other good gifts, gifts that he knows we need and will enjoy. Our job is to recognize these gifts, thank God for them, and enjoy them.

Questions

1. What is a future gift that everyone in God's family receives?

2. What are gifts that you have received from God?

3. Why does God give us gifts?

4. What should we do with all of the gifts that God gives us?

Digging Deeper

When picking out fruit to eat, there are certain criteria, including color, texture, and firmness, people look at to determine whether a fruit is immature or mature. Often Scripture uses the image of fruit to describe a person's spiritual maturity (John 15:8, Col. 1:10).

Look Up and Read Galatians 5:22-23

> *But the fruit of the Spirit is love, joy, peace, forbearance, kindness, goodness, faithfulness, gentleness and self-control. Against such things there is no law.*

The Apostle Paul, when describing part of the Holy Spirit's work, stated that the Spirit produces fruit in each of us. Interestingly, the word "fruit" that Paul used is a singular word, not a plural one.[16] Therefore, each of the characteristics that Paul described as the "fruit of the Spirit" is actually part of one fruit, not many. Therefore, every Christian will have all of the characteristics Paul described because they are all one fruit given by the Holy Spirit. However, every Christian will *not* be at the same level of maturity in each of these characteristics because maturity is based upon the receptivity of the Christian to the Holy Spirit's working in their lives.[17]

When someone becomes part of God's family, they receive the gift of the Holy Spirit (Acts 2:38). The Holy Spirit then works in a person to mature that person, ripening the fruit of "love, joy, peace, forbearance, kindness, goodness, faithfulness, gentleness and self-control" (Gal. 5:22-23a). As a Christian spiritually grows, this fruit continues to mature.

Christians will have *love* for each other and for the world. This is not the gushy, mushy, touchy-feely type love, but it is *agapē* love – the type of love that chooses to show love to someone.

They will also have a *joy* that does not depend on circumstances. This joy comes from understanding that, no matter what circumstances you may be in, you know that your relationship with God is permanent. This joy is a deep, lasting joy which the Holy Spirit gives to those in God's family.

The *peace* that one gets from the Holy Spirit is also not related to circumstances. There may be turmoil in your life, but God promises to work everything out as he wants it to be worked out (Rom. 8:28). Therefore, those in his family can have a deep peace, knowing they are resting in the loving hand of the Sovereign God.

The Holy Spirit also matures a believer by giving *forbearance*, which means patience, to that person. This patience helps us live through difficult circumstances with difficult people. Interestingly, the word patience in the Scriptures is most often used to describe the character of God as he deals with people![18] Therefore, as the Holy Spirit teaches us how to be patient with difficult people, we understand how patient God is with us as we repeatedly disobey him, demand from him, and refuse to thank him.

The Holy Spirit also matures our *kindness* toward others so that we can be truly concerned for others and deal gently with everyone.

Stemming from our moral uprightness, a mature *goodness* reaches out to others to actively show kindness. It is because of our mature *faithfulness* to God and others that we will be known as loyal and reliable.

The Holy Spirit also gives us a *gentle*, or meek, spirit as we understand that we must submit to God and allow him to teach us. Our *self-*

control also matures as the Holy Spirit teaches us to reign in our passions, controlling our anger and our tongue.

There is no Christian on earth who is a sparkling display of the completely mature fruit in these areas. However, the Holy Spirit is willing to continue the process of maturing this fruit in each of us. Are you willing? Are you teachable? Are you a beautiful, plump fruit ripening on the vine, or are you withering as a fruit that refuses to submit to the Holy Spirit's work?

Family Fun

Get an empty jar or bowl, some small pieces of paper, and something to write with. Take turns writing down gifts that you have from God. Remember "everyday" gifts such as air to breathe, eyes to see, patience, love, and beautiful color (God could have made everything black and white!) as well as other gifts such as the members of your family, talents, toys, and special events. After writing each gift on a separate piece of paper, place the paper in the container. Keep this container, extra paper, and a writing utensil in a public spot such as on your table or by your door. Then, whenever anyone thinks of another gift that God has given, write it on a paper and place it in the container. After a month, take out the pieces of paper and read them all. Thank God for all of the wonderful gifts that he gave you that month!

Teaching 7: Life is Hard

Review Theme Verse

Know that the LORD is God. It is he who made us, and we are his; we are his people, the sheep of his pasture. (Psalm 100:3)

Handing It Down

Digging Down

Let's read a story about Rylie:

* * *

Rylie tried to control her breathing and knocking knees. Breathe in. Breathe out. Breathe in. Breathe out. She stood at the starting line of her first big running race. Ahead of her stretched a path that wound through the leaf-strewn woods, across a wooden footbridge that spanned a small creek, through a grassy meadow on a hill, and finally to the flag-defined finish line.

As the shot of the gun rang through the air, Rylie sprinted from the line, claiming a great spot in the large pack of fellow runners. The first segment of the race was wonderful. Rylie easily glided through the woods, enjoying the fall colors of the leaves as she passed other runners who were already struggling for breath. "Wow, this is easier than I thought!" Suddenly, as she was passing another runner, she stumbled and fell to the ground, skinning her knee on a tree root. The other runner looked back and sneered, "Hah, got you! If you try to pass me again, I'll trip you again!"

Rylie stood up, her knee hurting and her spirits shaken. She had not expected others to try to stop her! She began running again, focusing not on the painful throb of her knee, but on the wooden bridge ahead.

As she approached the footbridge, she noticed that the ground was getting squishy. It then turned into a muddy mess where the water from the creek had overflowed the banks and made the ground a thick mud-soup. Sloshing through, she groaned as she worked hard to take every step through that sucking-mud. "Why in the world did I enter this race?" she questioned.

Finally she made it over the bridge and began the long climb up the hill. Her breathing got hard, and her leg muscles screamed that they had had enough. Rylie began to wonder if she should just drop out of the race. Then she began hearing the yells of the spectators. Instead of the cheering crowd that she expected to hear as she climbed the hill, she heard "Boo!" "Get out of the race!" screamed one spectator. By half-way up the hill her body and her emotions were exhausted as they fought her desire to give up and quit.

As she slowed down, she looked up and there, standing at the finish line, was her coach. "You can do it, Rylie," he yelled, "Don't give up." With her eyes firmly glued to her coach, Rylie kept running, one foot in front of the other, until she crossed the finish line and completed the race.

* * *

Look Up and Read Hebrews 12:1-3

> *Therefore, since we are surrounded by such a great cloud of witnesses, let us throw off everything that hinders and the sin that so easily entangles. And let us run with perseverance the race marked out for us, fixing our eyes on Jesus, the pioneer and perfecter of faith. For the joy set before him he endured the cross, scorning its shame, and sat down at the right hand of the throne of God. Consider him who endured such opposition from sinners, so that you will not grow weary and lose heart.*

God never promised that life would be easy. He never said that, because we are part of his family, we will always get what we want or that we will always feel happy. In fact, the writer of Hebrews compares our lives to a race that is difficult, just as Rylie's race was. As we try to follow God and live as God wants us to live, some people may try to stop us, make fun of us, or even say mean things about us. Circumstances may enter our lives that make us think that God must not love us. There may be times when we want to give up believing in Jesus and being part of God's family. We may even think of quitting the race.

However, just as Rylie looked up and saw her coach, we can focus on Jesus. We need to remember that we are part of God's family not because we get a wonderful life, but because we believe that God is real and that he deserves to be worshiped. We believe that Jesus died and forgave our sins, and we believe that we will live with God forever after we die. Life can be hard, but if we remember why we are part of God's family, then we will finish the race.

Questions

1. The writer of Hebrews compares our lives to what?

2. Does God promise that life will be easy?

3. Who can we focus on and think about when life becomes hard?

Digging Deeper

"I can't believe God allowed me to fail that test!" "What? I'm pregnant?" "How dare that police officer give me a speeding ticket!" All three of these situations are part of a group of trials that come as a consequence of our own actions. We should not be surprised if we fail a test because we did not study, get pregnant if we are sexually active, or get a ticket if we are speeding. There are consequences to actions, and sometimes peoples' lives are difficult because of the choices they make. However, not all difficulties stem from someone's bad choices.

Look Up and Read Hebrews 11:36-37

> *Some faced jeers and flogging, and even chains and imprisonment. They were put to death by stoning; they were sawed in two; they were killed by the sword. They went about in sheepskins and goatskins, destitute, persecuted and mistreated.*

Here we read of some difficult situations! Who were these people who were imprisoned, sawed in two, destitute, and persecuted? These were the chosen, beloved children of God! There are times when we think that, because we are Christians, we deserve to have a wonderful life, filled with money, health, and safety. After all, we are children of God, right?

Jesus stated, "In the world you have trouble and suffering, but have courage – I have conquered the world" (John 16:33 NET).[19] God does not promise that Christians will have an easy life. No, God actually says that sometimes he will allow us to go through trouble so that our faith becomes stronger.

Look Up and Read James 1:2-4

> *Consider it pure joy, my brothers and sisters, whenever you face trials of many kinds, because you know that the testing of your faith produces perseverance. Let perseverance finish its work so that you may be mature and complete, not lacking anything.*

Our reaction, when trouble comes, should be to run to God, asking for his strength, wisdom and courage to face the situation. When we do that, firmly believing God loves us even when there are trials, our faith deepens.

The Apostle Paul faced many hardships, including being stoned and left for dead, shipwrecked, and imprisoned (Acts 14:19, 2 Cor. 11:25, Acts 16:37). He was also given a specific "thorn" that he had to live with. When Paul begged God to take away this issue, God told him, "My grace is sufficient for you, for my power is made perfect in weakness" (2 Cor. 12:9a). After hearing this response, Paul could have gotten angry and listed all of the sacrifices he had made for God, demanding that God honor those by now removing this trial from his life. But he didn't. Instead he responded, "Therefore I will boast all the more gladly about my weaknesses, so that Christ's power may rest on me. That is why, for Christ's sake, I delight in weaknesses, in insults, in hardships, in persecutions, in difficulties. For when I am weak, then I am strong" (2 Cor. 12:9b-10).

Life is hard. We will all face situations that will make us angry, sad, confused, and frustrated. When we face those trials, we can either get angry with God, demanding that he fix the situation as we want it fixed, or we can run to God, asking for his strength and wisdom to face the situation. When we stay faithful to God throughout a trial, we will then bring glory to God and see his power work in our lives.

SECTION 6

DOCTRINE OF THE CHURCH

Overview

People use a variety of excuses for *not* being part of a local church. Perhaps you have heard some of these or even used them yourself. "I do not get anything out of the service." "I do not learn anything from the preaching." "I do not like the music they sing there." "The church is too big for me. I feel lost when I am there." "The church is too small for me. They do not have all of the programs I like to attend." Do you notice a common theme running through all of these excuses? I…I…I…I…

In many areas, churches are so abundant that people approach choosing a local church as if they are choosing a soda to drink. The focus is on their taste, on their preference. Church attendance may even be based on whether they have time to consume the product this week! Because their focus is on themselves, people minimize the church's purpose which is much bigger than meeting their preferences and perceived needs. Instead of having a me-focused attitude toward church, we should be God-focused.

Our theme verse for the Doctrine of the Church is from the book of Ephesians. "To [God] be glory in the church and in Christ Jesus throughout all generations, for ever and ever! Amen." (Eph. 3:21) The Greek word "doxa," which is translated "glory" means to "honor as enhancement …of status."[1] To give glory means to recognize someone's status or to make someone famous. Thus, according to this verse, one purpose of the church is so that God becomes famous throughout all generations, forever. (You will notice that this verse also states that one purpose for Jesus to be on this earth was to give God glory, just as it is a purpose of the church. We learned about Jesus' desire to make God famous in the Doctrine of Jesus.) Making God famous, not meeting our every preference, is the purpose of the church.

Do you complain about fellow Christians? Doing this affects the way people think of God. It gives Him a negative reputation because they see Christians as quarrelsome and judgmental. Is your attendance at a local congregation sporadic, based upon your own desires and schedule? If so, then you are not making God famous. Instead you are showing the world (and your family) that participation with others in his family to worship and learn about God is not as high of a priority as sports, shopping, or sleeping.

Making God famous is the purpose of the church, but too often the church is found in the headlines because of the immorality, dissension, and declining attendance within the family of God.

In the Doctrine of the Church we will examine what the church is and how, through the church, we can help make God famous. Although we will look at some benefits that we may receive from the church, we must remember that our theme verse indicates that one purpose of the church is to make God famous. May we learn how to make God famous together.

Theme Verse for Memorization: Ephesians 3:21

To [God] be glory in the church and in Christ Jesus throughout all generations, for ever and ever! Amen.

Let's learn about the church.

Teaching 1: What Is the Church?

Review Theme Verse

To [God] be glory in the church and in Christ Jesus throughout all generations, for ever and ever! Amen. (Ephesians 3:21)

Digging Down

What is the biggest church building you have ever seen? What is the smallest? Throughout the world there are many, many church buildings. Some have high ceilings and ornate gold decorations. Others are small, one-room meeting areas where people sit on benches or even on the floor. We call these places "churches." When we go to one of the buildings to worship God, we often say that we are going "to church." These buildings, however, are not the actual church of God. In fact, if every church building on the planet were destroyed, the church of God would still exist. What, then, is the church?

The church is not a building. It is not a place. The church is the people who are part of God's family.

Look Up and Read John 1:12-13

Yet to all who did receive him, to those who believed in his name, he gave the right to become children of God— children born not of natural descent, nor of human decision or a husband's will, but born of God.

When we believe Jesus died as a ransom for us, we are accepting God's gift, and we become his children. At this time we are made part of the church. As members of God's family, we *should* gather with our brothers and sisters who are also part of this family so we can listen to teaching about God and learn more about His Word, the Bible, together. While together we can sing songs praising God, pray, and help each other. It is necessary, as God's family, to gather together.

The preacher Paul, in a letter to his friend Timothy, said that he was writing so that all those with Timothy would understand how they should act in "God's household, which is the church of the living God" (1 Tim. 3:15b). The apostle Paul did not refer to the church as a building, but as a household, or family, of people. As part of God's family, we are called the church of God.

The next time you leave your house to go to a building where the church of God meets, instead of saying, "Let's go to church," say, "Let's go meet with the church!" It is very important that we gather with others of God's family because we are part of that family, the church!

Questions

1. What is the church?
2. How does one become part of the Church?
3. What could we say instead of "Let's go to church"?

Digging Deeper

What do you know about your ancestors? Were they from many different countries or just one? Where did they live? What were their jobs? What did they believe? There are many questions to ask about your ancestors, most of which cannot be answered. Even though you do not know every detail of their lives, you do know that you have ancestors. We each have a rich history because our ancestral family stretches back in time. They may have even crossed international boundaries.

The same is true with our spiritual family, the Church. When we are part of God's family we are part of a large group that spans time and national boundaries. Have you heard of anyone who is part of God's family and yet from a different time or place than you? Perhaps you thought of people like J.R.R.Tolkien, Corrie Ten Boom, or Billy Graham.[2] There are even people such as John Chrysostom, Stephen the martyr, and the Apostle Peter, who loved and served God centuries ago.[3] All of these people, spanning time and continents, are part of God's family, the church. The church is not just a local body of believers, it is made up of people from all over the earth, stretching back many centuries. This universal body is joined together under Jesus, its head.

Look Up and Read Colossians 1:18, 24

And he is the head of the body, the church; he is the beginning and the firstborn from among the dead, so that in everything he might have the supremacy. . . .Now I rejoice in what I am suffering for you, and I fill up in my flesh what is still lacking in regard to Christ's afflictions, for the sake of his body, which is the church.

Both of these verses refer to the church as Christ's body. Paul repeats the analogy of the church being like a body. He states that God "appointed him [Jesus] to be head over everything for the church, which is his body" (Eph. 1:22b-23a).

Do you ever feel lonely as a Christian? Does it seem as though all of those around you think differently than you do about who God is, who Jesus is, and what the Bible says? We are not alone on our Christian journey. We are part of an immense group of people, spanning time and the world, who have lived and sometimes died for their Christian beliefs. We are not alone.

Peter, one of Jesus' closest friends, wrote a letter to Christians who were scattered all over his known world. In it he encouraged them to live upright lives that brought praise to God. He assured them that they were not alone in what they believed. He encouraged them to take comfort in being part of an enormous group that he called "the people of God."

Look Up and Read 1 Peter 2:9-10

> *But you are a chosen people, a royal priesthood, a holy nation, God's special possession, that you may declare the praises of him who called you out of darkness into his wonderful light. Once you were not a people, but now you are the people of God; once you had not received mercy, but now you have received mercy.*

When we decide to follow God we become part of the people of God, the church. As a result, we are not alone; we are part of a huge group that has lived and died for their belief in Jesus.

Teaching 2: Why Be Involved?

Review Theme Verse

> *To [God] be glory in the church and in Christ Jesus throughout all generations, for ever and ever! Amen. (Ephesians 3:21)*

Digging Down

Have you ever fallen asleep in church? If so, do not worry, you are not the first person to do that!

Look Up and Read Acts 20:7-12

> *On the first day of the week we came together to break bread. Paul spoke to the people and, because he intended to leave the next*

day, kept on talking until midnight. There were many lamps in the upstairs room where we were meeting. Seated in a window was a young man named Eutychus, who was sinking into a deep sleep as Paul talked on and on. When he was sound asleep, he fell to the ground from the third story and was picked up dead. Paul went down, threw himself on the young man and put his arms around him. "Don't be alarmed," he said. "He's alive!" Then he went upstairs again and broke bread and ate. After talking until daylight, he left. The people took the young man home alive and were greatly comforted.

> Worship is not finally a matter of serving or satisfying human feelings, but serving and rightly glorifying God through song, proclamation, teaching and acts of mercy.
> - Thomas C. Oden[4]

There was a man, Paul, who knew about the Bible because he had spent quite a bit of time studying Scripture. Once, when he was on a trip, he and his friends stopped at the town of Troas. On Sunday they met with the church there, and Paul began teaching about the Bible. People were so eager to hear him teach that they stayed until midnight to listen! One young man got so tired that he fell asleep. What happened to this young man?

Can you imagine being so eager to hear someone read and teach about the Bible that you were willing to stay up until midnight? The people in Troas are a great example to us because they were very excited to meet together as a church so they could learn more. Reading the Bible together and hearing someone teach the Bible are two of the reasons why Christians should meet together (1 Tim. 4:13).

Some people think that reading the Bible by themselves is enough. They do not think they need to meet with others to hear someone teach about it. Think a moment. Would you trust yourself to fix your car? Most people, when their car needs to be fixed, take it to a mechanic who has studied cars. So, too, we should learn about the Bible from someone who has studied it. When we hear what someone else has learned about the Bible, we will learn more than if we just read the Bible by ourselves.

There are many other reasons to be involved in the church. The church is a place where you can get encouragement (Heb. 10:25). Getting together with our church family when we are feeling sad or lonely reminds us that we are not alone. The Bible tells about a time when Peter, one of Jesus' friends, was in prison. While he was there, the church met together and prayed for him (Acts 12:5). As part of a local church, we will have friends who desire to help us and pray for us!

We should gather with others in God's family to learn together, pray together, sing praises to God together, and encourage each other. When we do this, we will glorify God and be reminded that we are not alone. We are part of the church which is the family of God.

Questions

1. Why were the people in Troas staying up until midnight?
2. Explain reasons why we should want to meet with others who are part of God's family.

Digging Deeper

We all want to be loved, right? This might seem like an easy question. Of course we want people to help us, accept us, and even adore us! However, love is not just being accepted or being taken care of by an adoring fan. There are times when love can be very difficult to give, and love can even be very difficult to receive.

"If your brother or sister sins against you, rebuke them, and if they repent, forgive them," stated Jesus (Luke 17:3b). Jesus' statement contains two commands. What are they? Because we are God's children and part of his family, the church, we are called to both rebuke and forgive each other. Both of these can be very difficult to do.

How often should we forgive someone? Peter, Jesus' disciple, asked Jesus that very same question.

Look Up and Read Matthew 18:21-22

Then Peter came to Jesus and asked, "Lord, how many times shall I forgive my brother or sister who sins against me? Up to seven times?" Jesus answered, "I tell you, not seven times, but seventy-seven times."

Perhaps Peter had someone specific in mind when he asked this question. Maybe Peter had already forgiven that person seven times. Now he was just itching to write off that relationship and condemn the person as unforgivable at the next infraction. Jesus, however, did not give Peter that option. Instead, Jesus told him that there was no limit to the number of times he was to forgive someone. Paul later reiterated this when he wrote that love "keeps no record of wrongs" (1 Cor. 13:5d). Although forgiveness is sometimes difficult to give, there is no room in the church for anger and revenge (James 1:19-20). As members of God's family, we also have the responsibility of showing love by rebuking family members who are sinning.

Imagine hiking with your family, enjoying beautiful views from the mountain and valley below. Suddenly the trail veers to the left. If you do not stay on the trail, then you will plummet down into a ravine below. You look behind you and see two other family members laughing, obviously engrossed in a funny story. They do not see the turn in the trail. You debate. Should you interrupt the funny story that is being told to warn them of their mistake? Or do you let them enjoy their story which means they will fall to their death? Obviously you would warn them of their mistake.

We should have the same care and concern for our family members in the church.

Look Up and Read James 5:19-20

> My brothers and sisters, if one of you should wander from the truth and someone should bring that person back, remember this: Whoever turns a sinner from the error of their way will save them from death and cover over a multitude of sins.

When we see a fellow-Christian beginning to turn away from God and allowing actions or attitudes in their lives that are sinful, it is our responsibility to show them their mistake.[5] Beware, however, that you do so with love, first examining your own life so that you are not a hypocrite as you gently point out someone else's sin. Jesus warned, "Why do you look at the speck of sawdust in your brother's eye and pay no attention to the plank in your own eye?...First take the plank out of your eye, and then you will see clearly to remove the speck from your brother's eye" (Luke 6:41-42). People love to point out the mistakes of others, but we must first examine our own lives and make sure that our motive for confronting someone's sin is love, not pride or revenge.

The church should be a place of love, a love that is so deep that each of us in the family of God gives and accepts correction and forgiveness.

FAMILY FUN

Just as Peter's friends prayed for him, we can pray for each other! As a family make a list of people in the church who are having difficulty. Include people who may be struggling financially, physically, emotionally, or spiritually. Take turns praying for those on your list. Keep that list with your Bible or this devotional so that, as a family, you continue to pray for those who need God's encouragement and help. As you see answers to prayer, make a note of them. (Remember, answers may not always be what we want to happen. God may answer contrary to what we think is best!)

Teaching 3: The Enemy of the Church

Review Theme Verse

> *To [God] be glory in the church and in Christ Jesus throughout all generations, for ever and ever! Amen. (Ephesians 3:21)*

Digging Down

Let's read a story about Zach and his friend Evan.

* * *

Zach ran out of his house, shouting to his mom, "See ya later! I'll be back by supper!" He was excited; his mom had told him that he could go over to Evan's house to play. As he ran into Evan's backyard, he saw his friend hiding behind a tree, taking quick peeks to the other side of the trunk. "Who is he hiding from?" thought Zach.

Suddenly Evan jumped out and began waving the stick around at the air, obviously wielding it as a sword at an invisible enemy. Zach watched a bit more as Evan expertly pushed his foe behind a bush and then forced him onto the ground, holding the sword-stick onto his enemy's chest.

"You are no match for me; surrender or die!" declared Evan. Zach laughed, grabbed a stick from the ground, and went to join the fight.

"Watch out! There's another one coming for you!" he shouted as he attacked the invisible assailant.

* * *

Zach and Evan were pretending to fight an invisible war, and they were having fun playing. Did you know that we actually do have enemies we cannot see?

Look Up and Read Ephesians 6:10-17

> *Finally, be strong in the Lord and in his mighty power. Put on the full armor of God, so that you can take your stand against the devil's schemes. For our struggle is not against flesh and blood, but against the rulers, against the authorities, against the powers of this dark world and against the spiritual forces of evil in the heavenly realms. Therefore put on the full armor of God, so that when the day of evil comes, you may be able to stand your ground, and after you have done everything, to stand. Stand firm then, with the belt of truth buckled around your waist, with the breastplate of righteousness in place, and with your feet fitted with the readiness that comes from the gospel of peace. In addition to all this, take up the shield of faith, with which you can extinguish all the flaming arrows of the evil one. Take the helmet of salvation and the sword of the Spirit, which is the word of God.*

In these verses we are told to "be strong in the Lord" (v. 10) and to "put on the full armor of God" (v. 11) so that we can fight against the "spiritual forces of evil" (v. 12).

In our world we might think that only the things we can see are real. For instance, we know a tree is real. Why? We can see it. We also know that other people are real because we can see them. The Bible, however, often refers to beings that are real, but whom we cannot see.

For instance, the Bible says that angels are real, although people rarely see them. The Bible also states that God has a whole army which fights for him. Joshua met with the commander of God's Army to get the battle plan before they attacked Jericho (Josh. 5:14). Elisha's servant saw God's vast army protecting them when the King of Aram came to kill Elisha, even though God's army was invisible to others (2 Kings 6:17). There are many beings who worship God whom we cannot see.

There are also beings that we cannot see who fight against God. These beings, led by Satan, try to turn people away from God. They hate the church because the church is made up of people who love and worship God.

Although we cannot see these evil beings, they are just as real as trees and people. How do we fight against beings we cannot see? We prepare ourselves by putting on the armor of God, just as the verses in Ephesians 6 tell us. We do not need to be afraid, because we have our armor and we are on God's side, and God is more powerful than these evil beings.

Questions

1. Can we see everything that is real?

2. How can we prepare ourselves so that we do not fall when we are attacked by these evil beings? Read Ephesians 6:14-17 again to help you identify the "parts" to the armor of God.

Digging Deeper

And the devil, who deceived them, was thrown into the lake of burning sulfur, where the beast and the false prophet had been thrown. They will be tormented day and night for ever and ever. (Rev. 20:10)

We know the end of the story for the devil. We know that he will not win the cosmic battle that is taking place; we can be sure that God's power, love, and justice will triumph. However, the end has not yet come, and we are living on a battlefield.

The devil, Satan, uses many methods to deceive people so they turn away from God. Some of them are as forthright as demon-possession or outright worship of Satan. Other methods are more subtle. Causing doubts about the reliability of the Bible could be one. Another is encouraging selfishness so we use our time and resources to please ourselves instead of seeking first to glorify God.

Peter, one of Jesus' best friends, wrote, "Be alert and of sober mind. Your enemy the devil prowls around like a roaring lion looking for someone to devour" (1 Pet. 5:8). Satan does not care what method is used; he just wants the people in the church of God to stop desiring to glorify God with their lives.

Look Up and Read 2 Corinthians 11:3-4, 13-15

> *But I am afraid that just as Eve was deceived by the serpent's cunning, your minds may somehow be led astray from your sincere and pure devotion to Christ. For if someone comes to you and preaches a Jesus other than the Jesus we preached, or if you receive a different spirit from the Spirit you received, or a different gospel from the one you accepted, you put up with it easily enough. . . .For such people are false apostles, deceitful workers, masquerading as apostles of Christ. And no wonder, for Satan himself masquerades as an angel of light. It is not surprising, then, if his servants also masquerade as servants of righteousness. Their end will be what their actions deserve.*

What was the problem that Paul addressed? Apparently there were eloquent speakers who came to the church and began teaching wrong information about Jesus and how to be saved. Unfortunately, the church easily accepted these teachings. Paul, in his letter to the church in Corinth, admonished them not to listen to these false teachers.

Satan will use lies, and what appears to be wisdom, in order to pull people away from the truth of Jesus. Those who are in God's family must be careful to make sure that what we believe is in the Scriptures. Otherwise, we are allowing Satan to deceive us.

Another way Satan turns people from God is by cultivating dissension among the church of God.

Look Up and Read Ephesians 4:25-27

> *Therefore each of you must put off falsehood and speak truthfully to your neighbor, for we are all members of one body. "In your anger do not sin": Do not let the sun go down while you are still angry, and do not give the devil a foothold.*

Too often there is arguing in the church over issues such as the way a program is run or something as minor as the color of the carpet. Paul warned the church in Ephesus that they should work together as one body, not allowing fighting and quarreling among themselves. The devil, grabbing any opportunity he can, will use arguments in the church to turn people away from focusing on their purpose of worshipping God and making God famous.

How does your community view *your* church? Is God becoming famous in your community, or do people view Christians as quarrelsome, gossiping, dissatisfied individuals? Although we know that God is more powerful than Satan, we are living out part of a cosmic battle, and we must be certain that we are not giving Satan ammunition. By studying the Bible and living at peace with our church-family members, we will make sure that "Satan might not outwit us. For we are not unaware of his schemes" (2 Cor. 2:11).

Teaching 4: Your Duty toward the Church

Review Theme Verse

> To [God] be glory in the church and in Christ Jesus throughout all generations, for ever and ever! Amen. (Ephesians 3:21)

DIGGING DOWN

Take a piece of paper and draw a head on it (do not include the eyes, ears, nose, or mouth). Now, everyone take a turn and draw one part of the body on this person. You can add an eye, arm, leg, or whatever part you want, but add only one part. When everyone has had a chance to add one part onto the body, look at your picture. What is missing? If this were a real body, what physical problems would your person have because of the missing parts?

Did you know that many local churches today look a lot like the picture that you drew? No, they are not literally missing an eye, a foot, and some fingers, but they are missing some vital parts.

The Apostle Paul wrote a letter to a church in the city of Corinth comparing the local church to a body. He stated that each person should be involved in a local church group. This allows each person to use the unique gift God has given to help those who are part of that particular church. When one person refuses to be involved, then the church looks like a body without an arm, leg, or ear. Without that part, the church has trouble.

Look Up and Read 1 Corinthians 12:14-27

> Even so the body is not made up of one part but of many. Now if the foot should say, "Because I am not a hand, I do not belong to the body," it would not for that reason stop being part of the body. And

> *if the ear should say, "Because I am not an eye, I do not belong to the body," it would not for that reason stop being part of the body. If the whole body were an eye, where would the sense of hearing be? If the whole body were an ear, where would the sense of smell be? But in fact God has placed the parts in the body, every one of them, just as he wanted them to be. If they were all one part, where would the body be? As it is, there are many parts, but one body. The eye cannot say to the hand, "I don't need you!" And the head cannot say to the feet, "I don't need you!" On the contrary, those parts of the body that seem to be weaker are indispensable, and the parts that we think are less honorable we treat with special honor. And the parts that are unpresentable are treated with special modesty, while our presentable parts need no special treatment. But God has put the body together, giving greater honor to the parts that lacked it, so that there should be no division in the body, but that its parts should have equal concern for each other. If one part suffers, every part suffers with it; if one part is honored, every part rejoices with it. Now you are the body of Christ, and each one of you is a part of it.*

"But in fact God has placed the parts in the body, every one of them, just as he wanted them to be" (1 Cor. 12:18). God would like us all to be part of the local body, the church, and when we refuse to be involved in the church, we cripple the body because we are not using the gifts God has given us.

There are many reasons why people choose not to be involved with the church, but most of the reasons are selfish ones. They are based in the idea that the church must serve *me* and help *me*. Instead of approaching church with a me-attitude, we should think about the entire body. Are we crippling the local church because we refuse to be involved?

As a child it may be difficult to know what part you have in your church. Do you like to sing? Then sing with joy so that others can see your joy and be encouraged. Are you good with younger children? Perhaps you can help your mom or dad as they serve in the nursery.

What are your talents and likes? You can pray and ask God to use you in the church.

One thing that everyone can do is have a good attitude about going to meet with the church. When we grumble and complain about going, we are not helping the church, but we are making other people miserable and turning their thinking from God. When we meet with the church we want to encourage those around us and help the body.

Our attitudes and actions do affect the church, no matter how young we are. Because we do not want to hurt ourselves and cripple the church, we must choose to use our talents to help the body of the church be complete and whole.

Questions

1. What is the church compared to in 1 Corinthians 12:14-27 (the verses we read)?

2. What is one way that you can help the church?

3. Pray together, asking God to use each of you in the local church body.

Digging Deeper

It is a joy to be part of God's family, the church. Part of this joy comes from knowing that we will live with all of our Christian brothers and sisters forever. What a wonderful thought! However, our joy in being part of God's family is more than just a future hope. It also stems from knowing we are part of a connected family while living here on earth.

Together we can encourage each other, learn from each other, and worship our God. When we join this family, we no longer have to feel alone. We have become part of a world-wide, loving group. God has given us guidelines to employ so that each member of the family can experience joy.

As a family, we are to be unified, not allowing ourselves to be taken up with petty arguments based on our own opinions and desires. As James stated, "What causes fights and quarrels among you? Don't they come from your desires that battle within you?" (James 4:1) When we allow our own pride and selfishness to infiltrate our church family, we will have arguments amongst ourselves, and our joy in being part of God's family will diminish.

We are also to respect and submit to those in the church who teach us and have authority over us.

Look Up and Read 1 Thessalonians 5:12-13

Now we ask you, brothers and sisters, to acknowledge those who work hard among you, who care for you in the Lord and who admonish you. Hold them in the highest regard in love because of their work. Live in peace with each other.

Look Up and Read Hebrews 13:17

Have confidence in your leaders and submit to their authority, because they keep watch over you as those who must give an account. Do this so that their work will be a joy, not a burden, for that would be of no benefit to you.

In order for our teachers and pastors to have joy in their work, we must respect them and even honor their hard work as they seek to serve God and shepherd the church. (Elders and overseers in the church are referred to as shepherds in 1 Peter 5:1-3 and Acts 20:28-29.) It is a difficult task knowing that you are responsible for leading the church in their spiritual growth. We can help their job be a joy by supporting and encouraging those whom God has placed in that position.

Another guideline that God gave involves our own contributions to the welfare of the church. We are to use our talents to serve God so the congregation will be encouraged. We are also to use our finances to help the poor and to support those who are doing God's local and global work. There has been a tradition in the church, based on Abraham giving Melchizedek one-tenth of all of the plunder of a battle, to give back to God one-tenth of all of the money we earn.[6] Because of that tradition on tithing, one-tenth is a great guideline to use. However, God may ask you to give more than one-tenth!

Look Up and Read 2 Corinthians 9:6-13

> *Remember this: Whoever sows sparingly will also reap sparingly, and whoever sows generously will also reap generously. Each of you should give what you have decided in your heart to give, not reluctantly or under compulsion, for God loves a cheerful giver. And God is able to bless you abundantly, so that in all things at all times, having all that you need, you will abound in every good work. As it is written: "They have freely scattered their gifts to the poor; their righteousness endures forever." Now he who supplies seed to the sower and bread for food will also supply and increase your store of seed and will enlarge the harvest of your righteousness. You will be enriched in every way so that you can be generous on every occasion, and through us your generosity will result in thanksgiving to God. This service that you perform is not only supplying the needs of the Lord's people but is also overflowing in many expressions of thanks to God. Because of the service by which you have proved yourselves, others will praise God for the obedience that accompanies your confession of the gospel of Christ, and for your generosity in sharing with them and with everyone else.*

Although God does not promise us wealth in this world, he does expect us to give willingly, cheerfully, and generously from what we have. As we help the poor around us and support God's global and local work, we give thanks to God for all that he has given us. As a result, people will turn to God with praise.

We are part of a growing, world-wide church, and we can have eternal joy because of our membership in this family. Let's each shoulder the responsibilities that we have as part of the church. In doing so, we will foster joy for each member and make God famous together.

Handing It Down

Notes

Introduction

1. *Merriam-Webster Dictionary Online 2010*, "Doctrine," Merriam-Webster Dictionary, http://www.merriam-webster.com/dictionary/doctrine?show=0&t=1287676513.

Doctrine of the Bible

1. Theodore G. Stylianopoulos, *The New Testament: An Orthodox Perspective*, vol. 1: *Scripture, Tradition, Hermeneutics* (Brookline, MA: Holy Cross Orthodox Press, 2004), 40.

2. Versions using "inspired by God" include the New American Standard Bible and New Living Translation. The New International Version and the Amplified Bible are two that use the translation "God-breathed."

3. The earliest copies of the New Testament were written in Greek, so understanding the Greek words used is useful for understanding the meaning of the text.

4. "Pontius Pilate Inscription," Great Archaeology, http://www.greatarchaeology.com/Pontius.php.

5. "Dead Sea Scrolls – A Compelling Find," All About Archaeology, http://www.allaboutarchaeology.org/dead-sea-scrolls.htm.

6. The chart was adapted by Matt Slick, "Manuscript Evidence for Superior New Testament Reliability," Christian Apologetics and Research Ministry, http://carm.org/manuscript-evidence. Matt compiled the information from three sources: 1) *Christian Apologetics*, by Norman Geisler, 1976, p. 307; 2) the article "Archaeology and History attest to the Reliability of the Bible,"

by Richard M. Fales, Ph.D., in *The Evidence Bible,* Compiled by Ray Comfort, Bridge-Logos Publishers, Gainesville, FL, 2001, p. 163; and 3) *A Ready Defense,* by Josh Mcdowell, 1993, p. 45.

7. "Fog," Carl Sandburg, http://carl-sandburg.com/fog.htm .

Doctrine of God

1. Frederick William Danker, ed., *A Greek-English Lexicon of the New Testament and other Early Christian Literature,* 3rd ed. (Chicago: The University of Chicago Press, 2000), s.v. "δοξάζω."

2. "The Hanging Gardens of Babylon," The Hanging Gardens of Babylon, http://hanginggardensofbabylon.org/ .

3. Scripture quoted by permission. Quotations designated (NET) are from the NET Bible® copyright ©1996-2006 by Biblical Studies Press, L.L.C. http://bible.org All rights reserved. This material is available in its entirety as a free download or online web use at http://netbible.org/ .

4. *Merriam-Webster,* http://www.merriam-webster.com/dictionary/sovereign, s.v. "sovereign."

5. *NET Bible,* note of Isaiah 6:3. Notes taken from the NET Bible® footnotes, copyright (c) 1996-2006 by Biblical Studies Press L.L.C. All rights reserved. Used by permission from http://bible.org. This material is available in its entirety as a free download or online web use at http://netbible.org/ .

6. Ibid.

7. Donald N. Bastian, "Elements," *Light and Life,* (March-April 2001):10.

8. The illustration of a watch's complexity pointing to a creator,

and thus creations' complexity pointing to a creator was made famous by William Paley. William Paley, Natural Theology, 14th ed. (London: S. Hamilton, Weybridge, 1813), 3. You may find the book online at http://books.google.com/books?printsec=frontcover&dq=Natural+Theology+Paley&sig=-9sNiVngRdg2Yhb-aIAaEiMiBOY&ei=0EFlTeaSMYGB8gbHsNyiBg&ct=result&pg=PR1&id=UYBEAAAcAAJ&ots=dPKtzzjdAR#v=onepage&q&f=false.

Doctrine of Jesus

1. Doctrine of God, Teaching 5, "God is Eternal."

2. C.S. Lewis, *Mere Christianity*, Book II, Chapter 3, paragraph 13, http://lib.ru/LEWISCL/mere_engl.txt.

3. Later in the chapter (John 1:15, 29-30), John the Baptist indicates that Jesus is "The Word." This is why we can substitute the name "Jesus" for the name "The Word."

4. David Taylor, "Discipling All Peoples: Today's Imperative and the Vision of Tokyo 2010," *Mission Frontiers* 31:5 (Sept-Oct. 2009): 9.

5. Hippolytus, *On The Twelve Apostles, Where Each of Them Preached, and Where He Met His End*, ANF, Book 5, *Christian Library: Heritage Edition*, version 1 (Rio, WI: AGES Digital Library, 1997). Eusebius recounts the ministries and deaths of the apostles throughout his book, *The Church History of Eusebius*, Nicene and Post-Nicene Fathers, Second Series, Vol. 1 *Christian Library: Heritage Edition*, version 1 (Rio, WI: AGES Digital Library, 1997).

6. Michael Pidwirny (Lead Author); J. Emmett Duffy (Topic Editor). "Ocean". In: Encyclopedia of Earth. Eds. Cutler J. Cleveland (Washington, D.C.: Environmental Information Coalition, National Council for Science and the Environment).

[First published in the Encyclopedia of Earth April 7, 2010; Last revised Date September 10, 2010; Retrieved October 13, 2010 <http://www.eoearth.org/article/Ocean>].

7. "Mount Everest: The Highest Altitude," Geology.com, http://geology.com/records/highest-mountain-in-the-world.shtml .

8. Pidwirny, "Ocean," http://www.eoearth.org/article/Ocean .

Doctrine of the Holy Spirit

1. "About the Library: Fascinating Facts," The Library of Congress, http://www.loc.gov/about/facts.html .

2. Jonathan Edwards, *The Works of Jonathan Edwards*, vol 2, *Religious Affections*, Part 3; *Christian Library: Heritage Edition*, Version 4 (Rio, WI: AGES Digital Library, 2007), 853.

3. *A Greek-English Lexicon of the New Testament and other Early Christian Literature*, 3rd ed., s.v. "σφραγίζω."

Doctrine of People

1. Scripture quoted by permission. Quotations designated (NET) are from the NET Bible® copyright ©1996-2006 by Biblical Studies Press, L.L.C. http://bible.org All rights reserved. This material is available in its entirety as a free download or online web use at http://netbible.org/ .

2. Ibid.

3. Curtis Vaughan, Frank E. Gaebelein, ed., J.D. Douglas, assoc. ed., *The Expositor's Bible Commentary*, Vol. 11 (Grand Rapids, MI: Zondervan Publishing House, 1978), 216.

4. Scripture quoted by permission. Quotations designated (NET)

are from the NET Bible® copyright ©1996-2006 by Biblical Studies Press, L.L.C. http://bible.org All rights reserved. This material is available in its entirety as a free download or online web use at http://netbible.org/ .

5. Martin Luther, *The Schmalcald Articles*, Part 3, Article 1, Section 3; in the *Works of Martin Luther*; available from the *AGES Digital Library* (Rio, WI: AGES Software, 2007).

6. To review how Jesus' death paid for our sins, read the Doctrine of Jesus, Teaching 3.

7. To review the Trinity's role in our salvation, read these sections: God planned salvation – Doctrine of God, Teaching 7, Jesus paid for our salvation – Doctrine of Jesus, Teaching 3, the Holy Spirit assures us of our salvation – Doctrine of the Holy Spirit, Teaching 4.

8. "The 613 Mitzvot According to *Sefer Hamitzvot* of Rambam," Jewishvirtuallibrary.org, http://www.jewishvirtuallibrary.org/jsource/Judaism/613_mitzvot.html .

9. Ibid.

10. This command is taken from Deuteronomy 6:5.

11. The netbible.com Matthew 22:37, note 46. Notes taken from the NET Bible® footnotes, copyright (c) 1996-2006 by Biblical Studies Press L.L.C. All rights reserved. Used by permission from http://bible.org This material is available in its entirety as a free download or online web use at http://netbible.org/ .

12. These statistics are as of April 27, 2011. "Global Peoples Summary," Joshua Project, http://www.joshuaproject.net .

13. Ibid.

14. Ibid.

15. Ibid.

16. Paul originally wrote in Greek, and in that language there is a difference between the singular "fruit" and the plural "fruit". Therefore, even though in English we would say "fruit" both if we meant that we wanted one piece of fruit (singular), and if we were looking at the fruit of a tree (plural), in Greek there would be different words used for the singular and the plural.

17. John MacArthur, *The MacArthur New Testament Commentary*: Galatians (Chicago: Moody Press, 1987), 164.

18. Frank E. Gaebelein, ed., J.D. Douglas, assoc. ed., *The Expositor's Bible Commentary*, Vol. 10 (Grand Rapids, MI: Zondervan Publishing House, 1976), 498.

19. Scripture quoted by permission. Quotations designated (NET) are from the NET Bible® copyright ©1996-2006 by Biblical Studies Press, L.L.C. http://bible.org All rights reserved. This material is available in its entirety as a free download or online web use at http://netbible.org/ .

Doctrine of Church

1. *A Greek-English Lexicon of the New Testament and Other Early Christian Literature*, 3rd ed., s.v. "δοξα."

2. For more information on J.R.R. Tolkien, Corrie Ten Boom, or Billy Graham visit their websites: http://www.tolkiensociety.org/tolkien/biography.html; http://www.corrietenboom.com/history.htm; http://www.billygraham.org/biographies_show.asp?p=1&d=1 .

3. For more information on John Chrysostom, visit: http://

lectioecclesia.com/Chrysostom%2C-John-on-Thanksgiving-for-Suffering%2C-Homily-XXXIII-on-Hebrews.php, Acts 7:54-60 .

4. Thomas C. Oden, *Systematic Theology*, Volume 3 (Peabody, MA: Hendrickson Publishers, 1987), 284.

5. Matthew 18:15-17 gives the steps that should be taken when trying to point out someone's sin. First, you are to go to that person and try to show the error. If that person repents, your responsibility is over! If not, then you should take one or two other people who also want to help the person in error realize the error. If the one who is sinning continues, then the pastor and leadership at the church should be made aware of the sin.

6. We read of Abraham's gift to Melchizedek in Genesis 14:18-20, and the writer of Hebrews, in Hebrews 7:4-5 references this gift as a reason why we give one-tenth of our income back to God. We know that the tradition of tithing one-tenth is already established by Jesus' day because Jesus uses an example of a Pharisee who tithes one-tenth of his income (Luke 18:11-12).

Handing It Down

Index of Terms

A

Abraham 43, 67, 68, 180, 189
Ananias 105
Ascension 88
Attributes 31, 47, 52, 68

B

Balaam 114
Bastian, Donald 43, 184
Bezalel 114
Born Again 20

D

David 51, 71, 89, 107, 113, 114, 115, 134, 185
Dead Sea Scrolls 10, 11, 183
Disciple 147, 169
Doctrine IX, X, XI, XVII, XVIII, 32, 65, 66, 127, 161, 162, 183, 184, 185, 186, 187, 188
Doxa 161

E

Edwards, Jonathan 117, 186
Elisha 173
Eternal 2, 37, 39, 42, 48, 49, 50, 51, 52, 53, 55, 60, 66, 67, 68, 78, 80, 89, 90, 106, 107, 118, 141, 181
Eusebius 85, 185
Evidence, External IX, 8
Evidence, Internal IX, 12
Eyewitness 14

F

First Fruit 86
Frova, Doctor 9

G

Gideon 114
Glory XIII, 32, 36, 40, 42, 44, 48, 52, 56, 59, 79, 81, 89, 118, 125, 160, 161, 162, 163, 166, 171, 176
God The Father XV, XVII, 33, 34, 35, 36, 56, 79, 105, 106, 107, 108, 110, 111, 118, 130, 152
Grace 35, 58, 125, 159

H

Hanging Gardens 36, 184
Hippolytus 85, 185
Holy 41, 42, 43, 44, 56, 57, 73, 77, 100, 117, 122, 136, 166
Holy Spirit IX, X, XI, XV, XVII, 7, 8, 15, 16, 17, 18, 19, 33, 34, 35, 36, 103, 104, 105, 106, 107, 108, 109, 110, 111, 112, 113, 114, 115, 116, 117, 118, 119, 120, 121, 122, 123, 124, 125, 126, 139, 147, 153, 154, 155, 187

I

Illuminates IX, 15, 17, 19
Inspired 6, 7, 183

J

Jephthah 114
Jesus II, X, XV, XVII, 1, 2, 3, 5, 9, 10, 13, 14, 15, 19, 20, 23, 28, 29, 30, 33, 34, 35, 36, 39, 56, 57, 58, 60, 61, 65, 66, 67, 68, 69, 70, 72, 73, 74, 75, 76, 77, 78, 79, 80, 81, 82, 83, 84, 85, 86, 87, 88, 89, 90, 91, 92, 93, 94, 95, 96, 97, 98, 99, 100, 101, 102, 105, 106, 107, 108, 109, 110, 111, 112, 113, 114, 115, 116, 117, 118, 119, 120, 122, 123, 125, 130, 135, 137, 139, 141, 142, 143, 144, 145, 146, 147, 148, 149, 150, 152, 157, 158, 159, 161, 162, 163, 165, 166, 168, 169, 170, 171, 174, 175, 176, 185, 187, 189
Jonah 29, 148, 150
Joshua 29, 173, 187

L

Lewis, C.S. 68, 185
Library Of Congress 110, 111, 186
Luther, Martin 136, 187

M

Mariana Trench 100
Melchizedek 180, 189
Moabite Stone 12
Modalism 35
Mount Everest 100, 101, 186

N

Naaman 148, 150
Nebuchadnezzar 36, 37, 38, 40

O

Oden, Thomas 167, 189
Omnipotent 43, 107
Omnipresent 107
Omniscient 107
Original Sin 134, 135, 136, 138

P

Pacific Ocean 100
Paul 3, 4, 8, 15, 35, 48, 51, 84, 85, 86, 100, 113, 122, 139, 140, 152, 153, 159, 164, 165, 166, 167, 169, 174, 175, 176, 188
Peter 7, 8, 29, 105, 106, 119, 125, 165, 166, 168, 169, 170, 174, 179
Plato 11
Pliny 11
Pontius Pilate 9, 10, 39, 183
Priest 76, 77, 78

R

Ransom 75, 76, 78, 163
Reincarnation 140
Repent 22, 139, 168
Repentance 136, 139
Resurrection 56, 57, 82, 83, 85, 86, 114, 139
Revelation X, 29, 41, 42, 43, 52, 54, 70
Revelation, General X, 52, 54
Revelation, Special 52, 54

S

Salvation IX, X, 19, 56, 115
Samson 114
Satan 1, 15, 73, 74, 105, 173, 174, 175
Siloam 12
Sin 21, 22, 27, 43, 44, 45, 59, 60, 62, 63, 75, 76, 77, 78, 95, 96, 104, 109, 113, 117, 122, 132, 134, 135, 136, 137, 138, 139, 140, 141, 142, 148, 157, 170, 175, 189
Sinless 20, 75, 77, 78, 108
Solomon 121, 122
Son Of Man 75, 89, 90
Sovereign 37, 38, 39, 40, 89, 184
Stylianopoulos, Theodore 6, 183
Suetonius 11

T

Timothy 6, 29, 39, 152, 164
Trinity IX, 32, 33, 34, 35, 70, 106, 107, 110, 111, 118, 187
Truth IX, 2, 5, 66, 70, 74, 78, 83, 86, 90, 94, 96, 98

U

Unreached People Group 149

Authors' Bio

Photo by Mark Gobel

Tim Thurber graduated from Dallas Theological Seminary with a Master of Theology degree and currently serves as a pastor. Tami earned a Master of Arts in Theological Studies from Northeastern Seminary, and she has been involved in ministry to preschoolers, elementary age, teenagers, and adults.

Both Tim & Tami are certified instructors for the ministries of Walk Thru the Bible, SuperDoc, and UnveilinGlory; they also speak at retreats and other events.

Tim and Tami live in upstate New York with their three children.

CPSIA information can be obtained
at www.ICGtesting.com
Printed in the USA
LVOW01s0204130916
504363LV00014B/89/P